holds him in high regard for his professionalism, expertise, and integrity. His reputation for doing what's right is widely recognized and respected.

Mike not only guided us through the legal complexities but also provided invaluable emotional support during a difficult time. His professionalism, coupled with the respect he garners from peers and legal professionals, sets him apart in his field.

I wholeheartedly recommend Mike to anyone seeking legal representation. He is not just an outstanding attorney but also a genuine advocate for his clients' well-being. We are immensely grateful for his service and the positive impact he has had on our lives.

- T.W.

Michael and his legal team were a true lifeline during an incredibly difficult time. They were professional, honest, and compassionate throughout the entire process. They listened to my concerns, clearly explained each step, and made sure I felt confident in every decision. Thanks to their guidance, I was able to move forward and start a new chapter in my life. I highly recommend them to anyone in need of strong, supportive legal representation.

- R.C.

Michael and his team were wonderful to work with! The whole process felt very comfortable and friendly which is a huge plus when discussing major life decisions. He was so thorough—we discussed topics and made plans for things that I would have never thought to plan for. We are immensely grateful to have started our journey with FWLLS and I know that our family/ children will be too!

- S.H.

I can't thank Mike and his team enough for their help through my divorce. Facing such a difficult time, I was grateful for their compassionate and understanding approach. From our very first meeting, they took the time to clearly outline the entire process, setting realistic expectations and giving me a sense of control. Mike's communication was outstanding and he was responsive to every question I had. I felt he genuinely cared about my well-being. I would wholeheartedly recommend Mike Biederstadt to anyone in need of a caring and highly competent divorce lawyer.

- P.B.

Michael did a great job helping me with my estate plan! He is very professional and explains everything really well. I can tell that he really enjoys his profession. He is someone that I now will have a lifelong connection to, and I am confident that he will be an excellent resource to my family when the time comes.

- G.P.

I have trusted Michael and his partners and staff for over 5 years as my legal support. I am continually amazed by the sincere dedication Michael has to studying, researching, and advancing his knowledge in his field. He and his staff thrive on their clients' questions and any opportunities to be of support in making large and difficult life decisions more manageable. The levels of genuine and personal regard they have for their clients is simply unmatched!

- K.Y.

I cannot speak highly enough of the exceptional legal services provided by Mike throughout my family's challenging divorce and criminal proceedings. Mike displayed unwavering dedication and treated us with genuine care and compassion. He approached our case with a level of passion and commitment that exceeded all expectations. Mike truly treated us like his own family, ensuring our voices were heard and our rights protected every step of the way.

One thing that stood out about Mike was the respect he commands from everyone in the legal community. Judges, other attorneys, Guardian ad Litems—everyone he encounters

LIFE HAPPENS
ARE YOU READY?

LIFE HAPPENS

ARE YOU READY?

Everything You Need to Know
About Marriage, Divorce, and Estate Planning
to Protect Your Family, Finances, and Future

MICHAEL BIEDERSTADT, ESQ

ASCENDANT
MEDIA COMPANY

Life Happens. Are You Ready?
Everything You Need to Know About Marriage, Divorce, and
Estate Planning to Protect Your Family, Finances, and Future

Published by Ascendant Media Company
Chicago, Illinois, U.S.A.

ASCENDANT
MEDIA COMPANY

LAW / Practical Guides
LAW / Family Law / Divorce & Separation
LAW / Estates & Trusts

Editing: Carolyn Rowley and Storer Rowley
Proofreading: Dakota Nyght
Book Design: PearCreative.ca

Quantity Purchases: Companies, professional groups, schools, clubs, and other organizations may qualify for special terms when ordering quantities of this title.
For information, email info@fwlls.com.

HUMAN AUTHORED

Reg #: 4232083, authorsguild.org/human
Biederstadt, Michael, Author
Life Happens. Are You Ready?
Michael Biederstadt

Library of Congress Control Number: 2025927464
ISBN: 979-8-9939989-0-9 (paperback);
ISBN: 979-8-9939989-1-6 (hardcover);
ISBN: 979-8-9939989-2-3 (ebook).

To Kaia—my baby girl: You are the most joyful, enthusiastic, affectionate, caring, sweet, fearless, bold, and determined tiny human I have ever met. My tiny dictator—I love you!

And to the newest member of our family (Baby B #2): We haven't met yet, but I already love you more than you will ever know.

You two—your beautiful mother and our family—are my everything. This book is dedicated to you and to every parent who wants to protect their children, their family, and their future.

CONTENTS

FOREWORD

Every family law attorney has a moment when they realize the system is broken. For me, it came after nearly three decades of helping smart, successful people get divorced. I'd seen too many families destroyed, not by their own choices, but by a legal process that rewards conflict and punishes cooperation. I wrote two books about it. I built a law firm around a better way. And yet, in all that time, one question kept nagging at me: What if more of these families had been properly prepared before the crisis hit?

That's why I'm glad Mike Biederstadt wrote this book.

I met Mike several years ago through collaborative divorce cases we worked on together. In collaborative law, you see attorneys at their most exposed. There's no judge to hide behind, no procedural gamesmanship. Just two lawyers and their clients in a room trying to solve real problems in real time. That's where you find out what someone is really made of.

What I found with Mike was rare. During one particularly challenging case, we hit a wall. It was the kind of impasse where emotions run high and positions harden. Mike never made it about himself. He stayed calm, maintained his objectivity, and helped his clients work through their differences with the kind of steady, knowledgeable guidance that most people can only hope their attorney provides. That's not easy to do. It takes a lawyer who cares about the outcome for the family, not just the outcome of the case.

What sets *Life Happens. Are You Ready?* apart is its scope. Mike doesn't just cover divorce. He doesn't just cover estate planning. He connects the dots between marriage, divorce, estate planning, and financial protection in a way that most lawyers, even very good ones, simply don't. He shows you that these aren't separate legal events. They're chapters in the same story. And with proper planning, many of the worst outcomes I've witnessed in thirty years of practice could have been prevented.

If you're married, engaged, or building a family, this book is your playbook. If you're a professional or business owner with assets to protect, it's essential reading. And if you're the kind of person who solves problems before they become crises (the kind of person who does the research, who plans ahead, who refuses to leave their family's future to chance), then Mike wrote this for you.

Mike brings the same thoroughness, calm professionalism, and deep care for his clients to these pages that I've seen him bring to the conference room. Read this book. Share it with the people you love. And take action while life is good, because that's when the best decisions get made.

Raiford Dalton Palmer
Chicago, Illinois

INVITATION

To help you get started designing your life and your family's future, I've created some downloadable resources.

Visit:

www.fwlls.com/life-happens-are-you-ready

to get yours today.

PREFACE

Each morning we are born again.
What we do today is what matters most.

—BUDDHA

Before we begin, I'd like to celebrate you for taking the time to educate yourself on uncomfortable legal issues. The fact that you've picked up this book speaks volumes about your character. Although I may not know you personally, I already know something about you: *You care about your family's future and want to learn how to protect them.* I commend you. By simply picking up this book and educating yourself on life's most common legal problems, you are already further along than two-thirds of American adults.[1]

---

1 Victoria Lurie, "2025 Wills and Estate Planning Study," *Caring.com*, updated September 17, 2025, https://www.caring.com/resources/wills-survey.

It's unfortunate, but we all know someone who unexpectedly passed away too soon, became unable to take care of themselves, or went through an ugly divorce. But no one wants to imagine the possibility that it will happen to them. So we go about our busy lives and avoid thinking about these unpleasant, but all-too-common possibilities. In the end, most people wait until it's too late to educate themselves and do what needs to be done to protect their loved ones and avoid life's most common legal problems: death, disability, and divorce.

So, what exactly does it mean for you and your family to be legally protected? Let's imagine that you and your spouse don't make it home from date night...do you know what will happen to your kids? To your money? Your legacy? Do you know what your family will go through if you unexpectedly pass away, or are bedridden and in a coma after an accident? Do you know what typically happens if one day, out of blue, your spouse comes home and tells you they want a divorce? More importantly, are you prepared for these common problems, and do you know what you can do to minimize the damage?

As someone who has spent my entire career helping families answer these questions, I can tell you from experience...when these situations occur, it's not pretty. I've come to learn that life can change in an instant, and when it does, you don't want your family to go through the pain of discovering the answers the hard way.

When people invest the time to educate themselves on how the laws related to marriage, incapacity, and death affect them, and then take action to put a formal plan in place, they gain a tremendous sense of confidence and peace of mind. They are relieved to know that regardless of what the future holds, they will ultimately get the outcome they want, their children will be protected, and their life will be remembered as an example of a life well lived and wise preparation, rather than a cautionary tale of what not to do.

The purpose of this book is to give you the tools, strategies, and information you need to prevent your family from experiencing the unnecessary and often avoidable pain caused by life's most common legal problems: death, disability, and divorce. I've practiced law for over two decades, helping thousands of people navigate the ugly world of the legal system. During that time, I've witnessed every horror imaginable:

- I've seen siblings who once loved each other turn into bitter enemies over money and the need to control their parent's estate.
- I've witnessed children become wards of the state and get stuck in the system after losing their parents.
- I've fought in court to prevent parents from losing custody of, or even visitation with, their children to former in-laws after an ex spouse's death, all because of unfounded and false allegations.
- I've argued with hospitals to keep innocent children in the psychiatric ward, under twenty-four-hour surveillance, so they didn't succeed in their next suicide attempt,

stemming from years of mental abuse after being used as a pawn in their parents' custody battles.

- I've seen a parent take their life after losing their life savings and custody of their children in an unnecessarily contentious divorce.
- I've watched undeserving parents get visitation rights and even custody of their children after years of litigation, only to get a call from the police later, after the same parent has been arrested for selling drugs, attempted murder, abusing their children, or trying to drive their car off a bridge, with their toddler inside, while intoxicated.
- I've watched several forensic interviews of children who have accused their parent or siblings of sexual abuse.
- I've spoken to nurses after parents have been involuntarily committed to psychiatric hospitals after breakdowns resulting from the trauma of litigation.
- I've had clients get deported during their case, forced to leave the only home they've known for decades and their children without a mother or father.
- I've seen countless children grow up in the shadow of courtroom conflict and the effect it had on them later in life.
- I've watched families spend their life savings fighting each other in court, only to end up broken—financially, mentally and emotionally—when it's all said and done.
- I've witnessed spouses, who once stood at an altar in front of their loved ones and promised to love each other

"until death do us part," become strangers who can only communicate through their lawyers at $450 an hour.

- And I've seen what happens when people's life savings and estates are drained by endless legal fees, and how an adversarial legal system can leave nothing behind but a wake of financial destruction, stress, resentment, and regret.

When people fail to prepare, fail to plan, and fail to take control of their future, the result is always the same: pain, conflict, and loss in all areas of their life. When it comes to families, there are no winners in a courtroom. Your family's future shouldn't be left to chance, nor to the stranger sitting on the bench at your local courthouse.

In addition to seeing what my clients have gone through over the course of twenty years, I've learned these lessons myself, the hard way. That's why I've dedicated my practice to keeping families out of court, out of conflict, and in control of their future. It is my goal to educate and empower you to anticipate and avoid life's most common problems so you can prevent your family from suffering the same fate as my family and my clients.

WHAT IS POSSIBLE

It has been said that "luck is what happens when preparation meets opportunity"[2] and "good fortune happens when opportunity meets with planning."[3] Well, today is your lucky day, because fate and good fortune have brought us together. This is your opportunity, and the time to prepare is now. We cannot predict the future, but we can prepare for it. The average person only lives 26,061days,[4] and we only have so much time. If you aren't ready for what tomorrow may bring, your loved ones may pay the price. So, while we all should hope for the best, we must also prepare for the worst and plan for every possibility in between.

In this book, you will learn:

---

2 Seneca, Roman philosopher and stoic. This quote is often attributed to Seneca based upon his writings in a passage of *On Benefits* (Book VII, §1).

3 Thomas A. Edison. This quote is often attributed to Thomas Edison, along with the more detailed quote from the Thomas A. Edison Foundation that reads: "Unfortunately, there seems to be far more opportunity out there than ability…We should remember that good fortune often happens when opportunity meets with preparation." https://www.thomasedison.org/edison-quotes (2024 Edison Innovation Foundation).

4 "Life Expectancy at Birth (years)." World Health Organization (WHO), August 2, 2024. https://data.who.int/indicators/i/A21CFC2/90E2E48. The statistics vary across different sources, but according to the WHO, the average life expectancy worldwide is 71.4 years, or 26,061 days. Currently, the United States ranks forty-fifth among countries worldwide with a life expectancy of 76.4 years.

- **How to ask the right questions:** Learn what you need to know so you can begin to design the life and legacy you want and deserve.
- **How to properly prepare for marriage:** Review why prenuptial agreements are important, what discussions every engaged couple should have, and five steps you need to take to build a strong foundation for a successful marriage.
- **How to properly prepare your estate plan:** Familiarize yourself with the basics and learn about your options so you can confidently design a plan that will actually work to protect your family, wealth, and legacy.
- **How to properly prepare for the possibility of divorce:** Learn about the many options you have for ending your marriage and how to achieve a healthier, more efficient, and more dignified process. Alternative approaches to divorce can offer complete privacy and a quicker resolution, in addition to being much less expensive. Most importantly, these options are much kinder and less stressful for your kids.
- **How to find, interview, and hire an attorney:** Learn what qualifications to look for and how to find an attorney you can trust to represent your best interests, instead of their bottom line.

> Life happens to all of us, and if you aren't prepared for the possibility of your death, divorce, or disability, it could devastate your family. I want you to be ready for anything, not only for your sake, but for the sake of your children, your friends, your family, and your loved ones.

Whatever age or stage of life you find yourself in, I've provided an abundance of practical advice and information in this book related to marriage, estate planning, and divorce. Some of it may not be applicable to you personally, so feel free to choose your own adventure and focus on what applies to your family first. However, if any of your loved ones are in a different stage of life and any of this wisdom is applicable, please share the information with them so that together we can have a positive impact and protect the people we love and care about.

While I was writing this book, the words of best-selling author and inspirational speaker Simon Sinek stuck with me: "Give people what they want and they will like you for now. Give people what they need, and they will value you forever." So, with that in mind, let me be clear: This book is not merely an overview of applicable law and legal concepts. It is an attorney's guide to planning your life so you can achieve your financial, marriage, and parenting goals, to begin building a strong foundation for your family's future that will withstand any unexpected challenges that may come up along the way.

INTRODUCTION

BEEN THERE, DONE THAT, GOT THE T-SHIRT

The dictionary is the only place that success comes before work. Hard work is the price we must all pay for success.

—VINCE LOMBARDI

I am a recovering divorce attorney. For two decades, when people asked me what I did for a living, I reluctantly told them that I was a family law attorney, and then waited for the stereotypical joke, apology, or look of disdain that would follow. As a young man, and even now as I look back on my life, I never envisioned that this would have been my path.

From a young age, it was clear that a love for a good argument and constant negotiation was part of my DNA. As a kid, I was addicted to *Law and Order* and anything written by John Grisham. When I was nine, I snuck into the back of a movie theater to see Tom Cruise thunder away at Jack Nicholson and subsequently ran around screaming, "You can't handle the truth!" for months on end. My family will tell you that I was born to be a lawyer, and for as long as I can remember, I have been drawn to the law and wanted nothing else.

I went to school expecting to become the next Jerry Maguire.[5] After representing Olympic- and college-level athletes, helping to organize an NFL conference for agents and meeting Bob Costas, prosecuting Class X felonies as an extern for the Illinois State's Attorney's Office, clerking for a judge in Indiana, and submitting a memo that led to the Indiana Supreme Court Rules and jury instructions being changed statewide to limit discrimination during jury selection…I envisioned myself achieving greatness. Yet life doesn't always unfold as we imagine it will.

After graduating early from law school, I moved home to study for the bar exam and went to a few interviews. The country was in the early stages of a recession and my dream of becoming an NFL agent wasn't panning out, so I took a job with a local

5 Apparently, I really like Tom Cruise movies from the 90s, and I have now realized I'm old after being told that people won't get this reference. So, if you are too young to know who *Jerry Maguire* is, let me explain: In 1996, Tom Cruise played Jerry Maguire, a sports agent and the ambassador of Kwan, who had the entire US screaming, "Show me the money." If you've ever heard someone say, "You had me at hello," now you know where it's from.

family law firm. In my mind, it was temporary. It would give me courtroom experience, a paycheck, and most importantly, get me out of my parents' house.

THE REALITIES OF FAMILY LAW

For the first few years, life as a young family law attorney was exciting. There was never a dull moment, and the stories were unbelievable...threesomes gone wrong, strange fetishes, addictions, cults, mental illness, gut-wrenching abuse, suicide, criminal schemes, attempted murder, narcissism, and utter depravity. Like a gruesome car accident unfolding before your eyes, it was shocking, chaotic, and strangely intoxicating...until it wasn't.

Somewhere along the way, after years of being in the trenches of other peoples' wars day-in and day-out, it began to change me. The mind-blowingly crazy war stories stopped being entertaining at parties and became a weight I carried home, into my relationships, and into the hours I lay awake thinking about what waited at the courthouse the next morning. I was beholden to an endless to-do list and an unpredictable schedule, where a single email or telephone call could throw my entire day into turmoil. My reality had become spending holidays, vacations, and special events fielding vicious emails and petitions purposefully sent to ruin Christmas Eve dinner, New Year's Eve, or even the day of my wedding (when they knew I was getting married). Often, my phone would ring at all hours of the night, and I would pick it up to hear a crying voice or a police officer on the other end, detailing the latest parenting time violation, argument, incident of domestic violence, or suicide attempt.

My days consisted of consoling parents in the midst of chaos, from the mother whose kids were having a nervous breakdown because their dad told them the devil lived under her home and would kill them in their sleep, to the mom who was on her way to her ex's home to pick up her children because their dad was arrested for possession of cocaine and hiding 2,869 grams of cannabis gummies (286,900 bears, to be exact) in the family fridge. There was the New Year's Eve call from a mental hospital after my client was involuntarily committed because they were hearing voices from people hiding in the walls and found "their" access point in the sink. There were brake lines cut and sugar put in gas tanks on cars used to drive my clients' kids. One time, a client found a noose hanging on her second story balcony, which only Spiderman could've scaled. Then there was my favorite: During his weekend parenting time—while the kids were sleeping in a closet with no door in a studio apartment—Dad decided to go on Craigslist and invite other couples over to swing, as long as they brought drugs so his new wife would "lighten up." But my client (his ex) just so happened to be the swinger on the other end; she was desperately trying to prove what craziness was going on in the home and just so happened to identify a familiar and uniquely shaped appendage in the ad. I'll never be able to burn the Craigslist pictures out of my memory, or the visual I have of the judge almost throwing up when they were admitted into evidence.

After long nights in the office, I'd lie awake in bed thinking about my clients, what they were going through, and how to solve their problems. When I opened my eyes in the morning, I unconsciously began making my argument for the next court date. I couldn't shut it off, I couldn't get out of my own head, and I was losing my ability to separate my work from my personal life. It was an unhealthy way to live, and I was digging myself into an early grave.

On a regular basis, someone would jokingly ask how I stayed so skinny, and I'd tell them it was the stress diet. I was in a perpetual fight-or-flight mode, always in the midst of somebody else's war. It wasn't until I got a smartwatch that I realized my heart rate was so high, just while sitting at my desk, that I was effectively running a marathon on a daily basis.

I woke up one day and realized years had gone by, and I was no longer the optimistic and happy-go-lucky young man that I once had been. The constant stress and anxiety had taken a toll on me. It felt as if my entire life was now consumed with never-ending emergencies and conflict. I was surrounded by unhappy people going through the worst moments of their lives. Everywhere I turned, I was confronted with anger and argument, and I was constantly under siege and fighting with someone: the judge, the attorney on the other side of a case, and sometimes even my client.

Looking back on those days, it's hard to believe that was my life. In my twenties and thirties, I played the role of a lawyer, psychologist, detective, financial adviser, spiritual guide, and white knight. Don't get me wrong; it was heavy, but it was also extremely rewarding and led to some of my proudest achievements and most cherished relationships. My colleagues became mentors, and my clients became lifelong friends. I even cofounded a nonprofit with a former client to provide legal representation, counseling, court companions, and education to victims of domestic violence to help end the cycle of abuse.

Despite the chaos and constant stress, I was good at my job and enjoyed serving my clients in their time of need. One even referred to me as the "baby-faced assassin," which my wife still loves to joke about at parties. Yet, after years of representing countless wonderful and grateful clients, I could no longer see the good I was doing. I was miserable and losing my faith in humanity. When people praised me for my success, awards, or the nonprofit's work, I dismissed their kind words and could only focus on my dissatisfaction. Objectively, my life was fantastic, but I couldn't shake the gnawing feeling that life was passing me by and I was born for a greater purpose. In hindsight, it was because I was trying to live a moral, honest life and genuinely help people while attempting to navigate a broken legal system that was filled with and rewarded those who didn't.

When I started practicing law, things were different. For the most part, attorneys respected each other and were reasonable. The job wasn't personal; it was professional. It felt as if we helped people navigate a difficult time with dignity, respect, and reason. Gradually, over time, that began to change. Lawyers became more difficult and unwilling to settle cases outside of court and without a fight. I don't know if it was a shift in society, politics, the rise of social media, or if more lawyers simply realized they were billing at an hourly rate and could make more money by creating conflict among families.

Regardless of the reasons, it became apparent that no matter how much I genuinely cared about my clients and their families' best interests, it was not within my power to end their cases quickly. I was unable to negotiate reasonable compromises or stop their legal fees because I had no control over the process, the judge, the delays, or the other side. In most courtrooms, the rules weren't enforced. The simplest of issues took months to resolve and cost my clients thousands of dollars.

What bothered me most was that no matter how unreasonable or dishonest the other side was, it was extremely rare for people to be punished for their despicable behavior. And the dirty secret every lawyer knew was that people have to pay their attorney to ask for the other side to pay their fees, these cases take months to resolve, and there's no way to predict if they will even get back what it cost them to pay the lawyer to ask. In the end, families were often left bankrupt, financially, emotionally, and morally, because of the adversarial nature of the legal system. Even after we won, my clients felt as though they had lost because of the emotional damage and bill that followed.

CHARTING A NEW PATH

With every passing year, I grew more disturbed by my profession, so I began searching for a new path. I became fascinated with investing and discovered my passion for the stock market, immersed myself in personal development books, began meditating daily, started focusing on my health, and studied finance, philosophy, human nature, and communication and negotiation skills. I enrolled in courses, became certified in mediation, trained in collaborative law, and completed several estate planning mentorships. In short, I began doing anything and everything possible to mask my growing disdain for the court system and change my circumstances.

After several years of soul searching, I realized what I really wanted was to prevent as many families as possible from experiencing pain and suffering at the hands of an adversarial court system. I wanted to stop perpetuating the problem and find a solution that would allow me to be proud of the role I played in my clients' lives and the impact I had on them, while (selfishly) also creating a healthier work-life balance for my family. I wanted my interactions with clients to be positive, to create lifelong relationships where I served as their trusted adviser, preventing and solving their problems as opposed to being the cleanup crew after the damage was done, and having them dread calling my office to discuss the latest emergency at my hourly rate. To do that, I needed to find an alternative option, one that would help families change the status quo, and that would not only serve the greater good, but would leave a resounding impact.

During this process, I spent five years reading countless books and completing thousands of hours of trainings, certifications, and mentorships. This led me to the discovery that my experience in litigation and background in family law allowed me to see things differently. I realized that family law, probate, and estate planning overlap in more ways than I could have imagined. Yet, after speaking with countless attorneys about my ideas, it became apparent that they hadn't considered how these areas of the law impact one another. What I saw as obvious solutions that could be offered to clients to keep their families out of court and out of conflict had never been contemplated by the more experienced lawyers around me.

> It became abundantly clear that, with proper planning, a majority of the problems we encounter during divorce, incapacitation, or death could be prevented.

If people were simply educated, before marriage or as a young family, and if we discussed difficult issues and designed a legal plan as a team, establishing their wishes before anyone became unhappy, sick, or dead, countless issues could be avoided. They could make wise decisions for their family when life was good and they were in the right frame of mind to do so. Making those decisions and legally documenting them, coupled with ongoing guidance, would ensure they got the outcomes they wanted and that their families would never see the inside of a divorce or probate courtroom. With all of this in mind, I burned the bridges and stopped litigating. I rebranded and launched my firm in a new direction to prioritize this new family-centered approach to keep families out of court and out of conflict.

What sets me apart from the crowd and makes my firm unique is that I understand family law and estate planning, and I also have a passion for finance. That allows me to help clients plan for death, disability, and divorce by putting the right plan in place, and to provide ongoing support that shields them from the devastation and destruction of litigation. However, I wanted to impact more families than just the ones I see in my office. This book is a compilation of all the knowledge and advice I've used to guide my clients toward conflict- and courtroom-free resolutions, and I hope it will help you on your journey toward securing your family's future. Let's get started.

SECTION 1

START ASKING THE RIGHT QUESTIONS

Yesterday is gone. Tomorrow has not yet come.
We have only today. Let us begin.

—MOTHER THERESA

A pilot who takes off with no idea where he's going will eventually crash. It is essential to have a clear vision for the direction of your life and who you want to become because each day presents a series of choices. Some are big, others small, but any of them can forever alter your future. A split-second decision or simple dumb luck can determine if the stars align in any given moment and whether a meaningless choice leads to meeting your greatest love or your demise. Yet the truth is that small hinges swing big doors and the small decisions you make are building your life one day at a time, whether you mean to or not.

Seneca captured the same idea over two thousand years ago: "For one who does not know which harbor he is seeking, no wind is favorable."[6] This ancient wisdom is more relevant today than at any time in history because our modern day lives are all-consuming. We are bombarded on daily basis with a million things that are stealing our time and attention. The days, weeks, months, and years just seem to fly by. That's why it's vital to set your intentions, devise a plan, and do the work to design and create the life and legacy you deserve.

If you don't know where you are or the destination you intend to reach, there is no way to map out the best route. In fact, you may end up going the wrong direction and get lost along the way. Or, even worse, you might sit idle and stay parked while watching the world (and your life) pass you by. But when you define the end result you're after, and plan before you move, you become more efficient and far more effective.

It has taken me over a decade to learn, digest, implement, and experiment with the strategies outlined in this chapter so I could distill them into a few pages. Applying them to your situation will not only be helpful for weighing your legal options, but in all aspects of your life.

---

6 Seneca. (1920). *Epistles* (Vol. 2: *Epistles 66–92*; Ep. 71.3; R. M. Gummere, Trans.). Harvard University Press. (Original work published ca. 65 C.E.).

CHAPTER 1

DESIGN THE LIFE AND LEGACY YOU DESERVE

The quality of your life is determined by the quality of the questions you ask yourself.

—TONY ROBBINS

Life is a self-fulfilling prophecy of whatever is going on in your head at any given moment. As the old adage says, "Whether you think you can or you think you can't, you're right." It's just that simple. With the right attitude and a belief that you can successfully achieve what you want, you will be more inclined and motivated to take the necessary steps to succeed.

Naturally, that's easier said than done because we all have our issues—whatever those may be—but with some introspection and honest self-assessment, it's not hard to identify the patterns and recurring thoughts that consistently and subconsciously run through our minds. For me, it's that I never have enough time, I should've gotten more done, and I should be further along than I currently am. My wife worries about what could go wrong and is consistently tired. We've all got our own angels, demons, and defaults. The question is, what do those nagging (or encouraging) voices inside your head say to you on a daily basis?

As human beings, we are constantly asking questions of ourselves and those around us. Whether you realize it or not, those questions and the consistent thought loops running through your mind determine the direction and quality of your life. The questions that you ask yourself day in and day out do not arise by chance; they are deeply ingrained in your subconscious. They may stem from how you were raised, childhood experiences, relationships gone wrong, or a life-changing event, but we all suffer from the human condition, and these subconscious patterns were set in motion long ago without your knowledge. They are deeply rooted in who we are and how we view ourselves, our lives, and the world around us.

Dr. Daniel Amen, one of the world's foremost brain health experts, refers to these thought patterns as automatic negative thoughts (ANTs) and positive empowering thoughts (PETs). His analysis shows that, just like ants (the insects), our nagging, unconscious thoughts can quickly multiply and infest our conscious thoughts, in either a negative or positive manner.

We have the ability to logically and consciously discipline our minds, and in any given moment, we are presented with a choice about what to focus on—whether that's positive or negative—and who we want to be in that moment. The question is, are you consciously making that choice, or is it being made for you by your subconscious and unconscious automatic thoughts?

It is important that you are aware of these concepts and how they affect your day-to-day life. When we are under stress, we go into our own default mode: angry people get mad, fearful people get scared, anxious people worry, funny people crack jokes, optimistic people look for the silver lining, and pessimists envision the worst possible outcome. The question is, what is your default mode and emotional home?

Simply being aware of how your brain is wired and operates on a subconscious level will allow you to consciously and intentionally choose your thoughts and focus your attention more wisely. Understanding your thought patterns and learning to deliberately control your mind and focus is critical because your thoughts influence how you feel about your life. Your feelings determine your emotions. Your emotions then dictate your actions. Over time, your actions become habits, and those habits shape your values, beliefs, and view of the world around you.

My mission for this book is to inspire you to start asking the right questions and take ownership of your life, transform your future and the future of your family by shifting your focus to what you can control rather than what you cannot, remove fear and doubt about uncomfortable topics and the legal process, arm you with the tools, resources, and knowledge you need to confidently take action to design the life that you deserve, and set your family up for success—regardless of what the future holds—good, bad, or ugly.

But to do all of this, you must start with the end in mind and figure out what you truly want. So sit down, take a moment, and pretend it's ten, twenty, or thirty years in the future. Then, with as much detail as you possibly can, write down what you want to achieve, who you want to become, and the most magnificent version of your future that you can imagine:

- What does your life look like? Feel like?
- Are you married? To who?
- What is your relationship like?
- What do you/your spouse look like?
- How is your health?
- What do you do for a living?
- What's your salary?
- Where do you live?
- What does your house look like?
- What cars are in the garage?
- Do you have a pool? Hot tub? Sauna? Gym? Game room? Movie Theater? Basketball court? Helipad?
- How much money do you have in the bank? Retirement and/or investment accounts?
- What are your hobbies?
- What skills have you mastered?
- Do you travel? Where? How often?
- Do you have a vacation home? A boat? An airplane? A helicopter? An island?

- What awards and acknowledgments have you received?
- What are you most proud of and what defines your purpose in life?
- How many children do you have?
- Do you have grandchildren?
- Are they married? Happily? To who?
- Are they successful?
- What do they do for a living?
- Where do they live?
- Are you proud of them? Why?
- What qualities did they inherit from you?
- What family traditions have you passed down to your kids?
- What are your most cherished family memories?
- How are your relationships with your friends?
- What are you grateful for when looking back on your life?
- Do you have any regrets or things you wish you had done differently?
- What goals did you set for yourself, and did you achieve them? Most of them? All?
- When you're not in the room, what do you want people to say about you?
- How do you want to be remembered?
- What will your obituary say?

If you do this properly, by the time you reach the end of the exercise you should understand what you want to accomplish over the next five to ten years. From there, you should easily be able to create a step-by-step, actionable guide to what you are committed to doing on an annual, quarterly, and monthly basis to move you closer to your goals. The key is to have fun and enjoy the process. Treat it like a game. It should put a smile on your face. Envision yourself living the life you have designed, and relish that picture. Then take your list and put it in a place where you will see it regularly, commit it to memory, and go make it happen.

Countless studies have demonstrated the profound impact that goal setting and visualization can have on your life. It is a theme found in every self-improvement book, seminar, or coaching course on business or personal development. In one way or another, they all explain the importance of consciously and intentionally deciding on the outcome you truly want. Then, you need to get crystal clear on why you must achieve that outcome and how it will impact your life and the lives of those you love. They teach that reasons reap results. Before you begin focusing on the "how," you must figure out your "why" and motivation.

Once you know what you want and why, you're ready to devise your plan of action. Begin by brainstorming anything and everything that needs to happen to achieve your ultimate vision for your future. Consider who you need to become to reach your goals and who has already achieved what you are seeking and can help you along the way to speed up your progress. Then, take into account what could go wrong and how you can overcome any obstacles that may arise. Once you feel like you've got every idea out of your head and onto the page, take your list and begin to map out each milestone that must be completed to reach your destination. Then set definitive dates to accomplish each milestone while breaking them down into smaller, attainable benchmarks to measure your progress. The key is to commit to your vision by setting it in stone and documenting your goals so you can hold yourself accountable along the way.

I want you to apply this approach of designing your life to each chapter in this book. Regardless of whether you are single, married, a parent, young, old(er), rich, or poor, the information related to each stage of life should inspire you to start asking better questions and focus on what you truly want for your family, wealth, and legacy. In each chapter, you can take the examples I provide of common legal problems and apply the practical suggestions to your own life to avoid making the same mistakes. Along the way, I hope you get some insights that will help you improve individually and as a spouse or parent, even if you're not there just yet.

SECTION 2

ARE YOU READY TO GET MARRIED?

The most important decision you will make in life is who you choose to marry. This singular decision will have the greatest impact on the direction and quality of your future. What would it be worth to your family, friends, or children to know, before it is too late, whether their selection of a spouse is a wise choice or the biggest mistake of their life? In this section, you will learn about the discussions a couple must have before walking down the aisle, the importance of prenuptial agreements, and the five steps you need to take to have a successful marriage.

CHAPTER 2

ANSWERING THE IMPORTANT QUESTIONS ABOUT YOUR RELATIONSHIP

You are the average of the five people you spend the most time with.

—JIM ROHN

There's no greater feeling than meeting the love of your life and the excitement of a new relationship. It feels as if you can overcome any obstacle. You're blinded by faith and think that all you need for your relationship to succeed is love.

Unfortunately, over time, the elation and euphoria of the honeymoon period will fade. Attraction, passion, infatuation, and "love" are simply not enough to sustain a marriage over the long haul. When the real world becomes your day-to-day reality, and the rainbows and butterflies become dirty diapers, dishes, and dealing with in-laws, your marriage will need a solid foundation to stand the test of time.

I've witnessed thousands of couples going through divorce, and I have come to learn that a successful and lasting marriage is built on trust, common values, goals, and interests. If you and your spouse are aligned and on the same page, it results in a solid foundation for your relationship—a true partnership where you are in the trenches together, through thick and thin, good times and bad. A marriage where you have each other's backs, are heading in the same direction, have a shared moral compass and view of the world, and where you enjoy each other's company in the midst of the mundane along the way.

Above all else, healthy communication is the key to a great marriage. The day will come when an argument breaks out, chaos ensues, your patience is pushed to the brink, and you will question the future of your marriage. It is in the heat of those moments that your relationship will be tested. It will take maturity, respect, and a hell of a lot of self-control to **choose compromise and commitment over conflict**. In those difficult moments, which naturally occur from time to time in every relationship, it requires wisdom and patience to pause, take a breath, and acknowledge that **there is honor in admitting when you are wrong and finding a way to be honest without being hurtful**. Learning to listen, asking questions, and sharpening your problem-solving and argument diffusion skills will become invaluable. It's easier said than done, but who said marriage was going to be easy?

BUILDING THE FOUNDATION FOR A SUCCESSFUL MARRIAGE

There is a divorce in America every forty-two seconds. For decades, every marriage had a 40 to 50 percent chance of ending in divorce.[7] Interestingly, statisticians list a ton of factors that impact the likelihood of a marriage succeeding—including how

---

7 National Center for Health Statistics. "Marriages and Divorces." US Centers for Disease Control and Prevention. March 7, 2024. https://www.cdc.gov/nchs/nvss/marriage-divorce.htm.

National Survey of Family Growth. Various Publications through the US Centers for Disease Control and Prevention.

Jill Daugherty, Ph.D. "Trends in Attitudes About Marriage, Childbearing, and Sexual Behavior: United States, 2002, 2006-2010 and 2011-2013." March 17, 2016.

Copen, Casey Ph.D.; Daniels, Kimberly Ph.D.; Vespa, Jonathan, Ph.D.; and Mosher, William, Ph.D. "First Marriages in the United States: Data From the 2006-2010 National Survey of Family Growth. Division of Vital Statistics. March 22, 2012.

"Marriage and Cohabitation in the United States: A Statistical Portrait Based on Cycle 6 (2002) of the National Survey of Family Growth." Series 23, Number 28. (PHS) 2010-1980. U.S. Department of Health and Human Services, Centers for Disease and Prevention National Center for Health Statistics. February 2010.

Goodwin, Paula, Ph.D.; McGill, Brittany, M.P.P.; and Chandra, Anjani, Ph.D.; "Who Marries and When? Age at First Marriage in the United States: 2002." NCHS Data Brief No. 19. U.S. Department of Health and Human Services, Centers for Disease and Prevention National Center for Health Statistics. (June 2009). https://www.cdc.gov/nchs/nsfg/index.htm.

old you are when you get married, the state you live in, your level of education, your income, political affiliation, religion, and health, how long you dated, where you met, whether you lived together before marriage, the size of your wedding, how much you spent on the wedding, how affectionate you are in public, whether you have been married previously, and whether you have close friends or family members who are divorced.

The divorce rate has been falling in the United States since 1990. This is most likely due to millennials waiting until later in life to get married and living together beforehand. For instance, the divorce rate for people married between the ages of twenty and twenty-five is 44 to 60 percent. Yet, the data shows that people

---

Gillette, Hope and medically reviewed by Litner, Jennfer, PhD, LMFT, CST. "The Top 12 Reasons for Divorce." Psych Central. October 25, 2022. https://psychcentral.com/relationships/top-reasons-for-divorce.

Bieber, Christy, J.D. "Leading Causes of Divorce." *Forbes*. October 17, 2024. https://www.forbes.com/advisor/legal/divorce/common-causes-divorce.

Brolley, Brittany. "The Top Scientific Reasons Why Marriages Fail." The List. February 14, 2022. https://www.thelist.com/137677/the-top-scientific-reasons-why-marriages-fail/.

Smith, Sylvia. "5 Divorce Statistics & What They Say About Modern Relationships." Marriage.com. July 31, 2025. https://www.marriage.com/advice/divorce/divorce-statistics/.

"Divorce Statistics: Over 115 Studies, Facts and Rates for 2024." Wilkinson & Finkbeiner, LLP. https://www.wf-lawyers.com/divorce-statistics-and-facts/.

Steverman, Ben. "Millennials Are Causing the U.S. Divorce Rate to Plummet." Bloomberg. September 25, 2018. https://www.bloomberg.com/news/articles/2018-09-25/millennials-are-causing-the-u-s-divorce-rate-to-plummet.

Vuleta, Branka. "35 Encouraging Stats on the Divorce Rate in America for 2023." Legaljobs. May 20, 2023. https://legaljobs.io/blog/divorce-rate-in-america.

who get married after the age of twenty-five are 25 percent less likely to get divorced, and in fact, thirty-two seems to be the perfect age to get married.

The research also shows that, other than cheating on your spouse, incompatibility is reported as the top reason marriages end in divorce.[8] People who cite this reason reported a lack of shared values, marrying too young, sexual difficulties, religious differences, and other factors as reasons for divorcing.

I'll never understand how people can make such a monumental and life-altering decision without ensuring that they are compatible with their partner? After thousands of conversations with clients going through divorces about what went wrong in their marriages, I have come to the conclusion that people are not asking the right questions before they make the most important decision of their lives.

---

8 Amato, P.R., & Previti, D. (2003). "People's Reasons for Divorcing: Gender, Social Class, the Life Course, and Adjustment." Journal of Family Issues, Volume 24, Issue 5, 602-626. Sage Journals. https://journals.sagepub.com/doi/abs/10.1177/0192513X03254507.

Scott, S.B.; Rhoades, G.K.; Stanley, S.M.; Allen, E.S.; Markman, H.J. "Reasons for Divorce and Recollections of Premarital Intervention: Implications for Improving Relationship Education." American Psychological Association. Couple and Family Psychology: Research and Practice, 2(2), 131-145 (June 2013).https://pmc.ncbi.nlm.nih.gov/articles/PMC4012696/.

Stanley, Scott. "Reasons People Give for Divorce." Institute for Family Studies. April 10, 2017. https://ifstudies.org/blog/reasons-people-give-for-divorce.

"Survey: Certified Divorce Financial Analyst® (CDFA®) Professionals Reveal the Leading Causes of Divorce." Institute for Divorce Financial Analysts. 2025. https://institutedfa.com/leading-causes-divorce/.

Let's be honest, dating is basically a job interview where we present the most appealing version of ourselves. It takes months, if not years, before we start to reveal our true selves and let our freak flags fly. From bedside manners to bathroom behaviors, there's always something you're not ready to share at the beginning of the relationship. But even if you are lucky enough to truly know who your fiancé is before walking down the aisle, it still might not be enough.

THE BUSINESS OF MARRIAGE

Marriage is a legally binding and contractual agreement. In the eyes of the government, two individuals become a single entity. In essence, you are agreeing to form a joint partnership, just like a business. To succeed in marriage (or business), before you sign on the dotted line, you need to know the financial health of your partnership, what role each partner intends to play, whether your strengths and weaknesses complement one another, and if you are aligned on the goals you wish to achieve.

Unlike a business deal, it may be uncomfortable and awkward to ask your fiancé about their credit score, how much debt they have, or whether you can review their portfolio. Most young people do not have the forethought and self-awareness to have long-term goals and a twenty-year plan, let alone discuss them with their fiancé. They don't take time to have a sincere and candid conversation about how many children they want, how they intend to pay for them, and whether they both plan to work or if one wishes to stay home. They don't discuss how they want to raise their children, in what religion, or where they'd like them to grow up. They don't talk about what their financial or career goals are or how they would like to manage their finances. Yet, these conversations need to be had, and a lawyer (or therapist) can facilitate these extremely important discussions to ensure that the most important decision of your life is the right one.

I have encountered hundreds, if not thousands, of couples who could have easily identified these issues before strolling down the aisle and prevented their inevitable divorce. A few stereotypical examples of issues I've seen repeatedly that ultimately led to a couple's demise include:

- **Financial Responsibility:** One spouse discovering that the other was extremely financially irresponsible and has a mountain of debt, which they then spend years paying off, only to uncover even more hidden debt.
- **Parenting Duties:** Couples who realize they can't conceive, who don't want the same number of kids, or who realize far too late that they don't possess the parenting gene and can't handle raising a tiny dictator.
- **Religious Agreement:** Two spouses with different religious backgrounds expecting to raise their children in their own faith without discussing it, or even worse, discussing it but expecting their spouse to change their mind after the kids are born.
- **Geographic Location:** One spouse unilaterally deciding to move the whole family across the country to be near

their family or for work, and the other becomes miserable as a result.

- **Alignment of Lifestyle/Goals:** Marriages starting out as two-income households, but then one spouse stops working and no longer has the drive, motivation, and aspirations that they did at the start of the relationship.

PRENUPS

There's a common perception that prenuptial or premarital agreements are only for the wealthy and are offensive to even discuss, as if you are dooming the marriage before it has even begun. That perception is wrong. If you find the right professional, they can guide you through these awkward discussions. They can even provide you with questionnaires that you can simply fill out and exchange with your fiancé if you are too uncomfortable to have these necessary conversations directly.

Hundreds if not thousands of times, I have been told that engaged couples don't have anything (assets), so it isn't necessary to get a prenup. I strongly disagree. One day, they will have money, they may receive an inheritance, and the reality is that there's a chance they may get divorced. My experience tells me that few people know the legal ramifications of what will happen if they do end up divorced and how they could have prevented common problems when they still had the chance. It's not all about money though. A good attorney will help facilitate healthy discussions about the future of your marriage, children, and life together.

Please note that this advice isn't meant to push engaged couples into getting a prenup. The process can be expensive and sometimes painful. It's not necessary for *everyone*, but what IS necessary is that couples have these discussions to ensure they are making a wise choice when it comes to the most important decision of their life. These conversations can easily be had with a good questionnaire over a few cocktails, or they can be facilitated by a priest, counselor, therapist, or an attorney. The point and primary takeaway should simply be that you need to have these difficult, but important conversations before walking down the aisle.

So, how do you know if you need a formal prenuptial agreement and should go through the trouble of hiring attorneys before getting married? My advice is that if you have any doubts about your future marriage, then it may be a wise choice. It becomes absolutely necessary if:

- You have built up a reasonable amount of wealth before marriage;
- You own your own business;
- You have a stake in a family business;
- You own property jointly with someone else;
- You believe you're going to receive a large inheritance at some point down the road; or
- You and your fiancé plan to manage your money, assets, and affairs separately and you don't want to intertwine yourselves financially.

For some of the celebrities and high net worth clients I've represented, prenups were necessary because my client made significantly more money than their future spouse. The purpose was to prevent issues if they ever got divorced by contractually opting out of their state law and agreeing how much would be paid in spousal support, alimony, or maintenance (it is called different things in different states). Instead of using generic percentages that are applied to everyone to calculate the amount, they agreed to a much more reasonable, predetermined amount that factored in how long they were married and what assets they would receive if they ever got divorced.

Everyone's situation is different and for some, a formal prenuptial agreement is necessary. For others, a lot of problems can be avoided just by understanding your state laws and how to manage your property the correct way. What's most important is that you take the time to do your homework, consider your life circumstances, and have these conversations with your future spouse.

As you weigh your options before walking down the aisle, please ask yourself if you can put a price tag on the certainty of knowing that you are marrying the right person. How much would it be worth to be certain you're aware of your future spouse's finances, goals, values, and desires, and that the two of you have addressed how you intend to manage your household, marriage, and life together. I don't care if you have this discussion directly, through a therapist, or with attorneys, but for your own sake, please do, and encourage your children, family, and friends who are considering getting married to do so as well.

Now, don't get me wrong, most attorneys do not approach prenups the same way I do. Most simply focus every discussion on the terms of your future divorce. But that's not my style. I consider this a healthy exercise between couples. My role is not to create a problem for a happy couple by focusing on their potential divorce, but is instead to facilitate a discussion that will serve as the foundation for their family's future. During this process, I educate couples on the business of marriage and how certain financial decisions can drastically impact what would happen during a divorce, but it isn't the focal point. Divorce is a possibility though. In fact, there's a 40 to 50 percent chance of it happening, so why not discuss the elephant in the room and give it your best shot to prevent it from becoming a reality?

During your engagement, you have a unique opportunity and a free pass to ask some deeply personal questions, issue ultimatums, and open the door to some pretty serious conversations. The right professional or questionnaire can help guide your discussions and raise issues that you may never have considered. Regardless of whether you see a professional or not, my advice is to schedule a reoccurring meeting on your calendar, where you and your fiancé take a step back and some time to yourselves to enjoy the moment. It's busy and overwhelming, but your engagement and planning a wedding is supposed to be one of the happiest times of your lives. So, make it a priority to enjoy it and to enjoy each other. Schedule a weekly or monthly night out, a quiet night at home, a vacation, or a meeting with a professional. Pick a few topics and have a fun conversation where you dream about your future and discuss what you want out of life. Ask a lot of questions and dive deep. If you're both being open and honest, it'll be obvious whether you're on the same page and making the right decision to marry.

My wife and I developed the process that I now take my clients through during our own engagement. After reviewing dozens of marriage questionnaires created by therapists, we Frankensteined a ton of them together and I incorporated a few legal issues that needed to be discussed if we ever had to face divorce. We set some ground rules to avoid pushing each other's buttons, thoughtfully completed our answers, and shared them with each other. It was great! We had an extremely healthy discussion about our future, and it led to deeper discussions throughout our engagement regarding our needs, expectations, and ways that we could support each other to ensure we had a happy and lasting marriage. The promises we made to each other in that contract were personal, heartfelt, hilarious, and even risqué. Those conversations and our agreement solidified for me that I was making the right decision and that my wife and I shared common values, priorities, and goals for our life together.

Five Steps to Take Before You Walk Down the Aisle

1. Know What You Want:

Write down and then rank what qualities you value most in a spouse, partner, and best friend. If wealth and appearance are anywhere near the top of your list, please start over (and see a therapist). Then take that list and consider whether your future spouse exemplifies the qualities of your ideal companion.

If you want to make this a joint endeavor, take your list and add details describing what you admire most about your fiancé, along with any areas in your relationship that you would like to improve. Please do not use this as an opportunity to criticize, but rather an opportunity to have a respectful conversation about areas of improvement for the betterment of your marriage and future together. Then set some ground rules and share your answers. My advice would be to start with the positives. If your partner knows what's important to you in a relationship and what qualities you love most about them, they will be aware of how to bring more of that version of themselves to your marriage. Just remember, the goal of this exercise is not to get angry or defensive, but to gain a deeper understanding of your future spouse, what they want out of a relationship, and to determine whether you both are on the same page. As hard as it may be, the key is simply to listen. You want to learn how your partner honestly views your relationship and determine if it is built to make it for the long haul. We know that almost one out of every two marriages won't. So, before it's too late, it's worth taking the time and effort to find out if you are on the right, or wrong side, of who will happily grow old and gray together.

2. Map Out a Vision for Your Marriage and Future:

Both you and your partner should complete the exercises outlined in Chapter 1. Then have a heartfelt conversation to ensure you share the same goals, vision, priorities, and expectations for your marriage. Make sure that you address the issues of parenting, family values, residency, household responsibilities, career goals, finances, retirement, religion, political views, and anything else that may be important to you. If you aren't comfortable talking about this directly one-on-one, or it isn't going well, please seek the assistance of a professional.

Tip: Write everything down, date it, and put it in a safe place. Decades later you'll wish you had.

3. Healthy Communication:

Please educate yourself on healthy communication, problem-solving, and conflict resolution skills. These are invaluable skills to have when navigating marriage, parenting, business, and every relationship you'll ever have.

4. Education and Agreement:

You can educate yourself on the business of marriage and divorce with the assistance of an attorney or by investing time to research the laws and rules in your state. I highly recommend consulting an attorney because every state is different and this area of the law is complex. Many attorneys will provide a consultation for a small fee (or even for free) to earn your future business and help you determine if you want to move forward with a premarital agreement. There's nothing to lose. If you realize that you don't need a formal contract and you're okay with following your state law, it will cost no more than a night out for a nice dinner and you'll walk away with some good information. More importantly, you'll have a much better understanding of whether there's anything you and your future spouse need to discuss that you hadn't considered.

I often recommend that engaged couples interview attorneys together. Fair warning, this is not common and will likely throw the attorney for a loop because it's strange and unorthodox. They may even force you to sign a waiver. But regardless of how weirded out they may be by both of you showing up at the consultation, I recommend it for a few reasons. First, it gives you both an opportunity to get to know them and learn what to expect. But, more importantly, the attorney gets a chance to meet both of you and understand your goals. As an attorney, it's very difficult to humanize a name on a file when it is simply that and nothing more. It's important to get to know someone, hear their side of things, and put a face, a voice, a story, goals, and desires to that name. When we only hear about one person's experience and have no other insight, everything is left up to our imagination. It is also our job to prevent problems and we often make up issues that don't exist and never will. When an attorney hears both people's perspective, we are in a much better position to navigate negotiations and weigh the impact on the two human beings whose lives are being affected. The more we get to know you, the better we can gauge what the issues are, what you care about, what you want in your agreement, and more importantly what you don't and isn't necessary to address.

Second, it's important to ensure you're both comfortable with the attorney, their process, and that you jointly decide how to proceed. If you both know what to expect, and hear the same advice, explanation of the law, how those legal issues impact each of you, and break down your options, you can directly discuss and negotiate what it is that you want, as opposed to lawyers doing it for you. In the end, it can save you a ton of money in fees, allow you to take control of the legal process, avoid unnecessary arguments between lawyers, and alleviate a lot of stress at a chaotic time when you're worried about planning a wedding.

When researching potential attorneys in your area, you should focus on attorneys who are trained and certified in both mediation and collaborative divorce. They will have a more holistic and caring approach, while providing you with practical advice on how to handle any marital problems that may come up with as little cost and conflict as possible. They will know some great therapists in your area that you can reach out to if you ever need them. Trust me, it's much easier to have these conversations at a time when you can laugh about how it will never happen to you. If you are both educated on the business of marriage/divorce and understand the legal impact of your actions, you will be in a much better position to make wise decisions throughout your marriage.

After having these meetings, you should be aware of the attorney's background, process, and potential cost, and have a complete understanding of the law in your state regarding:

- The definitions of marital and non-marital property (along with community property, if you live in a community property state);

- The concept of gifting non-marital assets to the marriage, transmutation, and commingling of marital and non-marital property;
- How to handle your non-marital assets, any inheritance you may receive, and any business interests that you or your family have;
- How to handle marital and non-marital debts;
- How to best manage your finances based on your specific circumstances;
- How maintenance, alimony, or spousal support is calculated in your state and what your options are if you want to agree to something that is different from your state's default approach; and
- How child support is calculated in your state.

5. Deal-breakers:

After going through the exercises above, please consider what your deal-breakers are and whether there are any red flags that need to be explored before it is too late. For example:

- **How does your fiancé(e) treat strangers, animals, and children?** This says a lot about someone's character.
- **Do they have horrible relationships with any of their exes, family members, or old friends?** How people deal with others when their relationships break down is very telling about how they deal with conflict. You are no different, and they may treat you the same way in the

future. So please ignore what your future spouse is like when they are on their best behavior, and focus on what they are like when they are at their worst.

- **If you weren't in a romantic relationship, would you be friends?** Attraction fades, and thirty years from now, friendship will endure but looks won't.
- **Can you trust them completely? Do they have integrity? Are there any issues with dishonesty, infidelity, anger management, narcissism, drugs, or alcohol?** If you can't count on your spouse for support and if you don't trust them implicitly, RUN.
- **Do you have fun, share hobbies, and laugh together?** Couples that play together, stay together. To have a lasting relationship, you must enjoy each other's company and have common interests.
- **Do you enjoy spending time with their family and friends?** You will have to whether you like it or not, so get used to it. As you get older, your weekends are no longer your own, and you will inevitably spend a lot of time with your spouse's friends and family, especially if you have children. You may also want to take a serious look at your partner's family. To some degree, we are all products of our environment, and although we aren't destined to become our parents, it's likely that they have influenced and shaped who we are, how we deal with conflict, how we communicate, and how we treat our loved ones.

We offer our clients a premarital questionnaire to help them prepare before saying "I do." If you are located in Illinois, I invite you to book a consultation for more information. In addition, please check out our free resources at www.fwlls.com/life-happens-are-you-ready.

SECTION 3

ARE YOU READY TO GET YOUR ESTATE PLAN DONE?

Whether you realize it or not, you have an estate plan. Everyone does. If you haven't formally created a plan and aren't aware of what plan you have, the only question is, are you willing to run the risk of waiting to let your family find out for you?

In this section, as we explore how to protect your loved ones and get your estate plan done, you will learn:

- The basics of estate planning;
- The importance of designing your own plan, rather than accepting the default plan the government has in place for you (probate);
- The problems with probate;

- Your estate planning options;
- How to properly prepare for your potential incapacity and inevitable death;
- How to protect your children and the importance of emergency planning (in case you don't make it home);
- How to protect your assets and ensure they are inherited in the way you want, by who you want, when you want; and
- How to design the legacy that you will leave behind.

CHAPTER 3

WHY YOU SHOULD HAVE AN ESTATE PLAN

Only put off until tomorrow what you are willing to die having left undone.

—PABLO PICASSO

Whether we want to admit it or not, we are all going to meet our demise one day. Yet, based on my experience, what happens from a legal perspective after someone is incapacitated or passes away is one of the most misunderstood areas of the law.

THE FACTS

When it comes to the law, TV dramas, movies, and news reporters love to exaggerate and dramatize what happens. But real life doesn't play out the way it does on screen. Trials are boring and tedious, but thankfully, most people will never need to find out for themselves. The truth is that most people don't consult with lawyers or know the law. If they don't get arrested, sued, or commit a crime, they may never see the inside of a courtroom. That's why it's so important for everyone over the age of eighteen to educate themselves on the importance of estate planning and understand what happens during the court process—known as probate—because it is the only area of the law that will affect us all.

Fewer than one in four American adults have even taken the first basic steps to create an estate plan. When asked what would motivate them to do so, they reported:

- A medical diagnosis or health concern: 37%
- Purchase of a home or significant asset: 24%
- Family expansion (marriage, birth, etc.): 19%
- Retirement or an age-related milestone: 11%

According to a recent survey,[9] most people who don't have a Will or an estate plan in place, say the main reasons are:

- I haven't gotten around to it: 43%
- I don't have enough assets to leave to anyone: 35%
- It is too expensive to set up: 13%

---

9 Caring.com. A Guide to Estate Planning, "Wills and Estate Planning Study." https://www.caring.com/caregivers/estate-planning/wills-survey/.

*Please note that in the surveys conducted they allowed for multiple answers per response.

- I don't know how to get a Will or Trust: 11%

Does this sound familiar? My family, friends, and clients have given me the same excuses, and after speaking with many of them, I've concluded that people don't really understand the importance of estate planning. They don't know what makes up their "estate," or what will actually happen if they die or are incapacitated. They don't know what probate court is, or that **regardless of whether they die with or without a Will, their family is going to have to hire an attorney and go through probate**, where they will be in court for at least nine months, but usually for much longer. The average is nine to twenty-four months, but in some cases probate lasts for years. Most people don't know the difference between a Will and a Trust, how to ensure that their plan is maintained in a way that achieves their intended goals, or how much work their family will be required to do after they're gone based on which plan they have.

Estate planning can be a confusing and complicated subject. I get it…even after taking all my classes in law school and practicing as an attorney for more than a decade, I didn't know the importance of estate planning or the first thing about how these real-life scenarios played out in a courtroom. In fact, most attorneys don't unless they've experienced it firsthand. It was only after years of studying, taking courses, and getting hands-on experience that I began to fully understand this complicated area of the law.

So, if the importance and nuances of proper planning aren't common knowledge for attorneys that don't focus their practice on that area of the law, what chance does the public have? As you begin to educate yourself and get your estate plan done, you'll undoubtedly get a lot of conflicting advice from your family, friends, and the internet, which can be overwhelming and frustrating. So it's understandable if you've avoided getting your estate plan done. Thankfully, those days are now behind you. After finishing this chapter, you will understand the basics, what your options are, what you want, and the importance of getting a plan in place to protect your family, wealth, and legacy.

IT HAPPENED TO MY FAMILY

For me, estate planning is personal because my family has suffered from a majority of the stereotypical cautionary tales that attorneys warn people about. My grandfather died at the age of forty-two. Following his funeral, my grandmother told my mom that money had been set aside for her and her sisters. Years later, my grandmother got remarried, and after thirteen years of marriage to her second husband, she passed away. A few months later, my mom and her sisters received a small check from their stepdad, but everything my grandmother had when she died was jointly owned with her second husband. By law, he was entitled to everything, including my grandfather's death benefits. Upon his death a few years later, all my grandparents' money was then passed down to his children, while my mom and her sisters received nothing.

To this day, we have no idea what my grandfather or grandmother left behind. And twenty years later, it still stings and stirs up a heated conversation among my family. When discussing it with my mom as she looked back at old photos and thought about the death of her parents, she told me: "When my father died, it made me uncomfortable to discuss money. I was only twenty years old and didn't want to think about it. I wish I could go back in time and have a private conversation with my mom before she died so she could have explained what was left, what her plan was, and what she would have wanted."

It happened to my family. Could it happen to yours? I've personally cleaned out several of my relatives' homes, seen the accusations and infighting over personal property and outstanding loans, witnessed family disputes over relatives' end-of-life decisions that led to years of strained relationships, and had friends who passed away far too young, leaving their families to pick up the pieces. Please do not make the same mistakes that my family and friends have made by not getting a plan in place before it's too late.

We only have so much that we can control and plan for in life. You should take the necessary steps to design your family's future and the legacy you'll leave behind while you are healthy and life is good. We aren't promised tomorrow, and if today just so happened to be your last, would you have any regrets? What would you have done differently? How would you have spent your final days, moments, and breath on this earth? The last thing you want is to leave your children and grandchildren with unanswered questions for generations to come, or worse, resentment and a stain on their final memories of your life when they're left to clean up your mess because you failed to plan.

CHAPTER 4

AN INTRODUCTION TO ESTATE PLANNING

Most people fail, not because they lack talent, money, or opportunity; they fail because they never really planned to succeed. Plan your future because you have to live there! If you fail to plan, you are planning to fail.

—ROBERT H. SCHULLER

In my experience, legal concepts, the court process, and estate planning are completely foreign to most people. Statistics show that to learn complex subjects, repetition is necessary for us to retain information. So let's start with the basics and some of the biggest misconceptions about estate planning.

DO YOU HAVE AN ESTATE?

If you own anything, you have an estate. It doesn't matter how large or small it is, your assets are worth protecting, and it is up to you to properly plan and select the appropriate options for you and your family.

The assets that make up your estate are your:

- Home
- Bank accounts
- Investment accounts
- Retirement accounts
- Life insurance
- Vehicles
- Business interests
- Real estate (investment property, family farm, etc.)
- Personal property
- Jewelry, collectibles, art, etc.
- Any other property, assets, or possessions

DO YOU NEED AN ESTATE PLAN?

Everyone over the age of eighteen needs to have an estate plan. If you're young and you don't own anything, you minimally need Financial and Health Care Powers of Attorney that name someone you trust, who can step in quickly to access your accounts, pay your bills, manage your finances, and make health care decisions on your behalf if something happens to you. If you have a family, children, a home, or any financial accounts, at an absolute minimum you must have a valid and up-to-date Will and Powers of Attorney. Even if you think it is too expensive or don't believe that you have enough assets, the cost of not having an estate plan will most likely be significantly higher than having a lawyer prepare one for you, both financially and emotionally.

It is imperative that you decide who you want to raise your children, who you want to make decisions for you if you are unable to, and how you want your assets to be distributed. If you don't, your family may spend years and an astronomical amount of money in attorney's fees and court costs to clean up your mess. In addition, there may be trauma for generations to come if your family spends years fighting in court or if a judge decides your children should be raised by people you wouldn't have allowed to babysit them, let alone raise them.

What many people don't realize is that people with smaller estates may need planning even more than wealthy families. If a young mother and father of two with a small estate pass away, wasting $25,000 on expenses and attorney's fees is much more detrimental to their children's financial stability than it would be to a child from a wealthy family who is inheriting a small fortune. For a few thousand dollars, people with smaller estates can put a simple and straightforward plan in place to avoid probate entirely and get the results they want, while avoiding five to ten times that amount in fees. The value isn't the documents. Granted, they are important. But the real value is the specific and strategic coaching on how to title their property, properly set up their beneficiary designations, avoid probate, and if they have young kids, appoint guardians to raise them and manage their inheritance.

MISCONCEPTIONS

Next, let's address some of the false beliefs that people have about estate planning:

1. **"I don't have enough money or assets to leave to anyone":** It doesn't matter how much money you have. If you have kids or a family, you need an estate plan. A good plan will not only protect your family but will also address all the intangibles. It will provide you with a system to keep your finances organized and readily identifiable for your loved ones. A competent professional will provide guidance on which tasks you can easily do now but will be extremely difficult for your loved ones to address when you no longer have the ability to assist or provide them with guidance.

2. **"It's too expensive":** It is less expensive for you to design and draft an estate plan now than it will be for your family to go through probate. Additionally, if you wait, the attorney's fees will be much higher twenty years from now because of inflation. But more importantly, if something should go wrong in the meantime, the costs go far beyond money, and you can't put a price tag on your family's peace of mind.

3. **"I haven't gotten around to it, but I will":** Please don't wait until it's too late. Your legacy is at stake. It's wild how many times I have heard stories from people that the memory of their parent's life was scarred forever because of having to deal with their parent's estate.

THE THREE PHASES OF LIFE

In the world of estate planning, there are three phases of life that you need to be aware of: (1) when you're alive and well, (2) when you're alive but not well, and (3) when you die:

1. **When you're alive and well and life is grand**, you have the ability to prepare for the other two phases of life. You can legally sign estate planning documents, buy or sell a home, open or close bank accounts, designate or update beneficiary designations, and make medical decisions for yourself. Attorneys refer to this stage as when you have "capacity" to make legal decisions on your own behalf.

2. **When you're alive, but not well, and you're unable to legally care for yourself**, this is what we call "incapacity." Once you're incapacitated, you've lost the right to put a plan in place and legally sign documents, make health care decisions, or manage your assets. This is where powers of attorney, medical directives, and Trust documents come into play and can allow you to avoid probate court. But a Will has nothing to do with this phase of your life.

3. **When you die,** your powers of attorney and medical directives die with you. Any property that is owned solely in your name will need to be distributed to your heirs, and your family will be required to go to probate court to legally transfer ownership to your beneficiaries. In my experience, most people don't seem to understand that *where there is a Will, there is a probate.* Meaning, **if you only have a Will** at the time of your death, **your family will have to go to court** to gain access to your property. Your Will, however, does provide the judge with instructions on what you wanted, instead of deferring to the rules and laws of your state. **The only way to avoid probate completely when you die is to carefully manage every single thing you own or to properly transfer your property into a Trust.**

WHAT IS A TRUST?

In its simplest form, a Trust is an agreement between three people: (1) the "grantor," who creates the Trust and gives their assets/property to (2) the "trustee," who holds the assets/property for the benefit of (3) the "beneficiary."

To avoid boring you with the history of King Edward III, feoffees, and King Henry VIII[10, 11], conceptually, it may help to envision one of the earliest uses of Trusts: Imagine a medieval priest or knight leaving on a dangerous journey to faraway lands with no way to communicate with anyone at home. They would give someone they trusted control to manage their estate while they were away, and if they didn't come home, to take care of their family and household.

To further simplify this, for 99 percent of us, your only focus and what you will be putting in place is what we call a Revocable Living Trust (RLT). When you create an RLT, you are playing all three roles: You give your property to the Trust, which you control, for your own benefit.

While you are healthy, you can go about your life as you always have, and nothing will change except for the name on your statements. But if you are incapacitated, someone you've chosen steps into your shoes as a trustee to protect and manage your property on your behalf. And if you die, your trustee follows the instructions in your Trust, which directs them on what to do with your property after your death.

---

10 Hannay, A. J. "The Origins of the Statute of Uses." In *Law and Constitutional Change: Essays in Legal History*, edited by Norma Dawson, David Capper, and Conor McCormick, 27–43. Cambridge: Cambridge University Press, 2024. https://doi.org/10.1017/9781009797733.004.

11 David J. Seipp, "Trust and Fiduciary Duty in the Early Common Law." *Boston University Law Review* 91 (2011): 1011–1036.

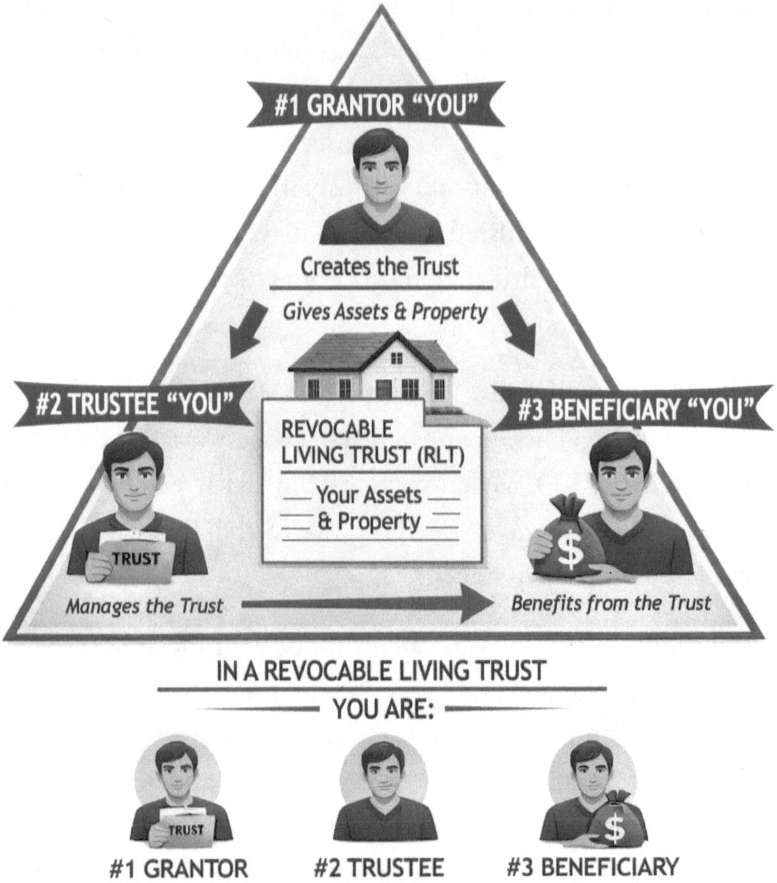

Trusts can avoid probate and keep your personal and most private information completely out of the public record. Trusts can help your family minimize or completely avoid taxes and outstanding debts, protect and keep money in the family in the event of remarriage, preserve government benefits for the elderly and people with special needs, provide asset protection for your loved ones by shielding assets from creditors, lawsuits, divorce, and bankruptcy, and ultimately, Trusts can ensure that your assets pass to who you want, when you want, in the way you want.

My favorite analogy for explaining a Trust is that you should think of it as a backpack. While you are well, you can put all your treasures in it, take anything out and play with it whenever you want, and it is a safe and convenient way to carry everything you own around with you. When you are no longer able to carry the backpack, you can simply put it down, and whomever you've chosen as a successor can pick it up, sling it over their shoulder, and continue in the direction you have instructed them to go.

WHAT IS PROBATE?

To clear up any confusion, probate courts have jurisdiction over a few areas of the law:

- When you are alive but can't make your own medical or financial decisions, you will be declared incapacitated. A legal case will need to be filed, and a probate court will appoint a guardian or conservator to make decisions for you and manage your finances. This is what we call guardianship or conservatorship.
- After you die, a petition will need to be filed in court to open a probate to administer your estate. The court will appoint and supervise your representative or executor, who will "marshal" your assets, meaning they will be required to locate, take control of, and value your assets.

They will also be responsible for paying your expenses, debts, and taxes, and then distributing what's left of your estate. This is what we call probate.

- If your children are under the age of eighteen, they aren't permitted to make their own legal decisions, own property, or enter into contracts. So, a legal case would then have to be opened on behalf of your children. We call this a minor's guardianship. The court will name a legal guardian, who will raise your children and have legal authority to make decisions on their behalf (*the guardian of their person*). The court may also appoint someone to manage their finances (*the guardian of their estate*). Depending on where you live, the court may require that any money or assets left to your children be frozen in a restricted account. Your children's guardian may be required to pay for a bond every year until they turn eighteen, which serves as an insurance policy just in case they steal your children's money. They may also be required to file an accounting with the court every year to account for every penny that is spent of your children's estate. If their funds are restricted, they will also have to ask permission to gain access to these funds. Both of those situations require your children's guardian to hire a lawyer, pay attorney's fees, and divert their time and attention away from your kids.

The term "probate" is used interchangeably for these three areas of the law and stages of life. In theory, a married couple could go through four separate probate cases, one for each spouse's incapacitation and subsequent death. If they have underage kids, there could possibly be a fifth. We will go a bit deeper into incapacity planning and how to protect your kids later in the chapter. So for now, let's focus on the most well-known form of probate: after someone passes away.

> Probate is required when a person dies with a valid Will (testate) and when a person dies without a valid Will (intestate), if they own any property solely in their name at the time of their death without a named beneficiary. Most people mistakenly believe that a Will keeps your family out of court altogether, but as you now know, ***your family must go through probate whether you die with or without a Will.***

The simplest way I've learned to explain this is that if you die without a will, you've left no instructions for the judge. In that case, the government's default plan will apply and a judge will make decisions for you. If you die with a Will in place, you've left instructions for the judge on what you want them to do. If you die with an estate plan, including a Trust that you've managed well, there's no need for a judge or court process at all. Probate is a voluntary court process and an unnecessary tax on your loved ones that you can easily avoid through Trusts, beneficiary designations, deeds, joint ownership of assets, and strategic planning.

WHAT'S THE PROBLEM WITH PROBATE?

You might wonder why I'm emphasizing the need to avoid probate. Here's why:

1. **Probate invites conflict:** Anyone who is angry, upset, or who simply wants to cause trouble is entitled to their day in court. They can easily challenge a Will or Guardianship Nomination, make outlandish allegations, and cause problems, all of which leads to additional expense and delay for your family. As a general rule, whenever people are in court, it invites conflict, so by avoiding probate altogether, troublemakers won't even get the opportunity.

2. **Probate is public:** Anyone who wants to can easily get a copy of the most personal details about your life, injury, death, assets, and what happens to your kids. A simple search online will reveal some of your favorite celebrities' or historical figures' Wills, how much money they had, and who they left it to. You can also find all the details about the legal fights their families had. To see what I'm talking about, do an online search for the probate cases or Wills of any of these people:

    - **Prince:** In 2016, Prince Rogers Nelson died with an estate worth \$156.4 million. When he died, all his assets were immediately frozen, and George Lopez had to loan his family \$20,000 so they could bury him in a small service and travel to get there. After six years of probate, \$87.24 million was spent on taxes, fees, and other expenses, and only $68.76 million was left for his family.[12]

- **Robin Williams:** Following his death in 2014, his third wife and three children were involved in a contentious probate battle over his $100 million estate. Within his estate plan, Robin left his home to his wife and his personal property to his children, but unfortunately he didn't provide enough detail and specificity. A fight then ensued over expenses for the home and the items in it, everything from awards, memorabilia, wedding gifts, and watches to a bicycle.[13]
- **Aretha Franklin:** After her death in 2018, a legal battle ensued until 2023, when a jury found that a 2014 handwritten Will found under Aretha's couch was her most recent and valid Will, instead of a 2010 Will found in a locked cabinet. In the end, after paying

12 Mission Wealth. August 10, 2022. Andrew Kulha. "Lack of Estate Planning Cost Prince's Estate Roughly $87 Million." https://missionwealth.com/probate-cost-princes-estate-millions/. TMZ. May 1, 2016. "Prince: George Lopez Helps Family With Big Bucks." https://www.tmz.com/2016/05/01/prince-george-lopez-money-family/.

13 *Forbes*, February 3, 2015, Danielle and Andy Mayoras. "Robin Williams' Widow Starts A Court Battle – But Why?" https://www.forbes.com/sites/trialandheirs/2015/02/03/robin-williams-widow-dishonors-his-trust-by-starting-court-battle/ LA Times October 2, 2015, Julie Cart, "Widow, children of Robin Williams settle dispute over his estate." https://www.latimes.com/local/lanow/la-me-ln-robin-williams-estate-settled-20151002-story.html.

expenses and fees associated with the legal case, her estimated $80 million was valued at $6 million.[14]

- **James Gandolfini:** When he died in 2013 at the age of fifty-one, his $70 million estate was not protected by trusts, and as a result, his family had to pay over $30 million in taxes, which could have easily been avoided.[15]
- **Jimi Hendrix**: In 1970, at the age of twenty-seven, Jimi died without a Will, and his family and bandmates have been in ongoing legal battles ever since.[16]
- **David Bowie:** Following his death in 2016, all the details of his $100 million estate, detailed in his Will, were made public for the world to see.[17]
- **Howard Hughes:** Following his death in 1976 without a Will, his $2.5 billion fortune led to one of the most

---

14 *BBC News*, July 10, 2023, Sam Cabral, "Aretha Franklin sons fight over will found under sofa." https://www.bbc.com/news/world-us-canada-66158755.

15 *Forbes*. July 20, 2013. Robert W. Wood. "6 Estate Planning Lessons From James Gandolfini's Will."https://www.forbes.com/sites/robertwood/2013/07/20/key-lessons-from-james-gandolfinis-will/. Investment News. July 23, 2014. Liz Skinner. "Gandolfini heirs will likely end up in court over giant tax bill: Lawyer." https://www.investmentnews.com/ria-news/gandolfini-heirs-will-likely-end-up-in-court-over-giant-tax-bill-lawyer/52574.

16 *Medium*. May 29, 2018. Peter Allsopp. "Jimi Hendrix Ongoing Estate Litigation." https://medium.com/@injudiciouslex/jimi-hendrix-ongoing-estate-litigation-c16c39f81692.

17 *Rolling Stone*. January 30, 2016. Daniel Kreps. "Details of David Bowie's Will Revealed." https://www.rollingstone.com/music/music-news/details-of-david-bowies-will-revealed-41117/.

infamous probate cases in US history, lasting thirty-four years.

- **Thomas Kinkade:** As a famous artist, Thomas had amassed over $66 million. Following his death in 2012, a battle ensued between his estranged wife and girlfriend over which of the two Wills he had prepared were valid.[18]
- **Groucho Marx:** One of the most famous examples of elder abuse played out in the public during a long battle between Groucho's children and his daughter-in-law.[19]
- **Britney Spears**: Without a doubt, this was the most publicized conservatorship dispute in history, which reportedly cost Britney over $30 million in attorney's fees.[20]

3. **Probate offers no protection:** Your assets will first be used to pay court costs, attorney's fees, debts, and taxes. What's

---

18 *Los Angeles Times*. December 24, 2012. David Ng. "Legal Battle Over Thomas Kinkade Estate Settled." https://www.latimes.com/entertainment/arts/la-xpm-2012-dec-24-la-et-cm-thomas-kinkade-estate-settled-20121223-story.html.

19 Groucho Marx Productions, Inc. v. Day & Night Co., 523 F. Supp. 485 (S.D.N.Y. 1981) https://law.justia.com/cases/federal/district-courts/FSupp/523/485/2298298/. *The New York Times*. February 6, 1983. Judith Cummings. "Bank and Ex-Actress Battle Over Groucho Marx Gifts To Her." https://www.nytimes.com/1983/02/06/us/bank-and-ex-actress-battle-over-groucho-marx-gifts-to-her.html.

20 *The New York Times*. April 26, 2024. Liz Day and Lauren Herstik. "Britney Spears and Her Father Settle Legal Dispute Over Conservatorship." https://www.nytimes.com/2024/04/26/arts/music/britney-spears-jamie-spears-legal-fees-conservatorship.html/.

left is given to your family outright, meaning that your spouse and children will take ownership of your property, but it won't be protected from creditors, predators, lawsuits, bankruptcy, or divorce.

4. **Probate takes time:** In the months and years following your death, when your family members are grieving, they will be tied up in court and dealing with attorneys, for an average of nine months to two years. Depending on what state and county you live in, the time frames may vary, but it will be a minimum of nine months.

5. **Probate Causes Delay:** After someone dies, their account is frozen when their bank is notified of their passing. Their loved ones will need money to pay for their funeral, burial, and to maintain their bills, but they won't be able to access their money for at least a few months. Then, even after getting access, they'll be required to file a public accounting of anything that is spent while in court. It's a double whammy because those who need the money most after the death of their spouse or parent will pay a great deal more in attorney's fees to ask a judge for permission to get access to the funds.

6. **Probate is expensive:** Even after you've already paid for a Will to be prepared, your family will still have to pay for court costs, bond fees, appraisal fees, attorney's fees, executor fees, and more. The costs will vary depending on what state you are in, but national studies report a range of 2 to 8 percent of your gross estate is lost to these fees. To put that

in perspective, if your estate is valued at $1,000,000, the statistics show that probate could cost your family anywhere from $20,000 to $80,000.

The best explanation I have heard about the cost of probate is: "Property passing through the probate process acts like water traveling through a leaky pipe. Every few feet, some of the water escapes, and at those spots there is always someone to collect the leakage. When it reaches the other end of the pipe—where the heirs collect—there is not always a whole lot left."

The explanation goes on to say: "Leaving property outright to loved ones through a Will is like pouring a pitcher of water into your cupped palms to take a drink. Most of the water falls on the floor, except for a few drops that you may be able to sip or lick off your fingers. Most of it disappears before it can be properly used."[21]

The good news is your family doesn't need to go through probate. Probate is optional and a voluntary court process. But if you want to avoid probate, you must take action now to create a comprehensive estate plan and diligently maintain it over time.

21 *Loving Trust* (Revised Edition), Robert Esperti and Renno Peterson, New York: Viking, 1994. Pages 10, 32.

WHAT ESTATE PLAN DO YOU HAVE?

As I've mentioned, everyone has an estate plan, even if they don't realize it. The question is whether your "plan" (or lack thereof) is the right one for your family and whether it will accomplish your goals. So, let's explore which estate plan you have:

1. **The Government Default Plan:** When you don't have valid legal documents, your state laws and a judge will control what happens to you when you are disabled, incapacitated, or die:

    - **If you become incapacitated**, your family will have to hire an attorney to go to probate court. **A judge will determine who will make medical and financial decisions for you and who will take care of your children**. Whoever is appointed may need to obtain a bond, which is basically an insurance policy to protect your assets if they are stolen or squandered. If they qualify for the bond, they will need to keep records of all the money that is spent and file an accounting with the court annually.
    - **If you die without a plan *(intestate)***, your family will have to hire an attorney to go to probate court. A judge will appoint a representative to collect, account for, and value your assets, pay your debts, and then provide your family with what is left of your money and property. Depending on your state law, **your estate will be divided 50/50 between your spouse and your children and given to them outright**. If

your spouse dies with you and your kids are minors, the judge will also decide who will raise your kids. **When they turn eighteen, they will get your entire life savings handed over to them to spend however they want.**

2. **A Joint Tenancy *(Beneficiary)* Strategy:** Any of your assets that are owned jointly with someone else (typically your spouse) will automatically pass to the joint owner upon your death. In addition, any assets with a named beneficiary will also automatically pass to whomever you've chosen upon your death. Common examples of assets that pass in this manner are joint bank accounts, homes, life insurance, and retirement accounts. These assets do not need to go through probate if you have your account ownership and beneficiary designations set up properly. Yet there is a lot of risk in relying solely on this type of planning. It should only be considered as a part of your overall planning strategy because you're losing a lot of benefits, and if not done correctly, this type of planning can fail or cause catastrophic and unintended consequences.
3. **A Simple Will Plan:** If your plan is done properly, you will have prepared for incapacity by selecting who can access your accounts and manage your finances *(Financial Power of Attorney)*, make medical decisions for you *(Health Care Power of Attorney or Proxy)*, and who will care for your kids *(Guardian Nomination)*. If your loved ones have access to these documents, know

their responsibilities, and you've given your financial and health providers a copy of your documents in advance, you can avoid unnecessary delays and fees if you're ever incapacitated and need a guardian to step in. After you die, Will planning follows the same probate process as the default plan, but the judge will follow your instructions instead of your state's law. In addition, you can opt out of a few of the unnecessary legal requirements for your family during probate, like paying for a bond, which is a waste of anywhere from a few hundred to a few thousand dollars depending on the size of your estate.

4. **Revocable Living Trust Plan *(RLT)*:** This is the most effective and strategic form of estate planning. Most people believe that Trusts are only for the rich, but that is simply not true. The cost won't be much greater than creating a Will, and in the end, the attorney's fees to go through probate will cost much more. When you have an RLT prepared, all the previously referenced documents will also be prepared, and your Trust will control and be the foundation of your entire plan.

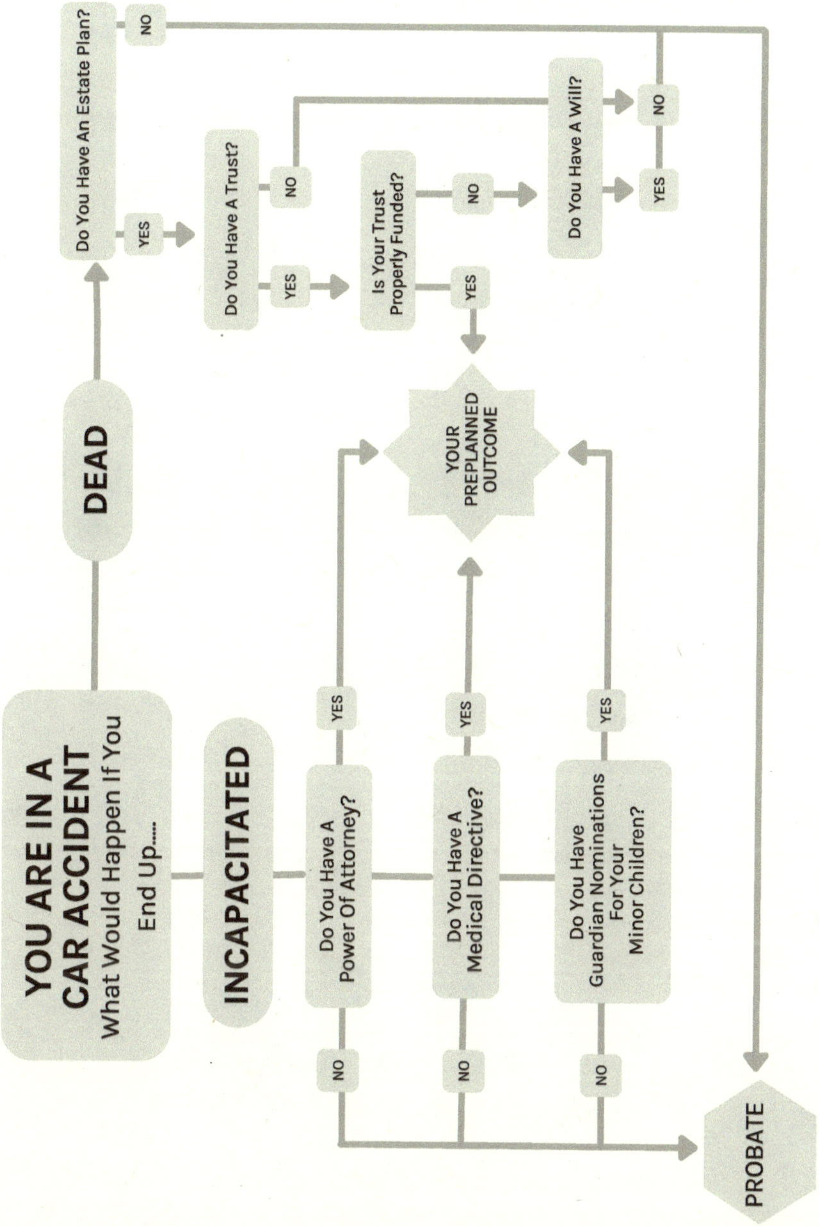
YOU ARE IN A CAR ACCIDENT
What Would Happen If You End Up.....
DEAD
Do You Have An Estate Plan?
YES
NO
Do You Have A Trust?
YES
NO
Is Your Trust Properly Funded?
YES
NO
Do You Have A Will?
YES
NO
YOUR PREPLANNED OUTCOME
INCAPACITATED
Do You Have A Power Of Attorney?
YES
NO
Do You Have A Medical Directive?
YES
NO
Do You Have Guardian Nominations For Your Minor Children?
YES
NO
PROBATE

CHAPTER 5

WHAT ARE YOUR PLANNING OPTIONS?

Life is what happens while you are busy making other plans.

—JOHN LENNON

No two estate plans are created equal, and the documents you receive from one attorney to the next will never be the same. It's not like buying a phone or a blender, where your only consideration is price and you can get the same exact product no matter where you buy it. We live in a consumer society, and we have been programmed to focus on cost when making our buying decisions. In most situations, we instinctively believe that the place offering a product the cheapest is the best option.

When it comes to estate planning, nothing could be further from the truth. That's what's so difficult about educating the public. People seem to believe that handling their plan should be simple and straightforward, and that anyone who went to law school should know how to do it. Take it from me, as someone who has read hundreds, if not thousands, of estate plans, that is simply not true, and there is a drastic difference between a cookie cutter, copy and paste, plug and chug your name into a generic document plan versus a customized, personal, and thorough plan prepared by an experienced professional who knows what they're doing.

When it comes to estate planning, your options are endless. Some are safer than others, and some will cost a significant amount more. In the age of artificial intelligence (AI) and online options, you can choose to invest your time, educate yourself, and give DIY planning a shot, or you can invest your resources and pay a professional for assistance. But who you choose becomes extremely important as well. Let's take a deeper look at each option.

ONLINE (DIY) PLAN

There are a lot of people who think they have a valid estate plan and have mentally checked off the estate planning box. They went online, answered a few questions, and in minutes they were provided with standardized and generic legal documents for a small fee. Considering only one in four Americans has a Will, if this is all you can truly afford, I support taking this initial step for the sake of appointing guardians for your children. However, my experience with my friends, family, and clients is that they trusted the directions on a national website, followed the prompts, and didn't take the time to do their homework. They didn't research their state laws, learn about all the documents they need and how to sign them properly, or figure out how to implement their plan after signing. In the end, most of the DIY plans I've reviewed were invalid because they didn't have everything needed, and even if they did, they weren't filled out or signed correctly. After I show clients why their documents aren't worth the paper they're printed on, they then curse the website for not being clear or spelling out the next steps.

People are also exploring using AI platforms to act as their personal lawyers. Before I explain why that concerns me, let me be clear: I am not opposed to technology. I have witnessed the transition from rotary phones to the first car phone, pagers to cell phones, floppy disks to hard drives, and the dawn of the internet age, and I fully acknowledge and admit that the development of AI is amazing. In seconds, vast and complex documents or code can be written by programs that are evolving at lighting speed. I do not fear technology and have embraced that AI is now an important part of our day-to-day lives and is great at certain tasks. However, as an attorney, I can tell you that when it comes to drafting legal documents, they're just not sufficient. Eventually the models will improve, but even when they do, AI is still merely a tool that is only as good as the user. It answers questions and gives you what you ask for, but if you don't know what to ask or what you're reading, it may not work out very well. An AI document will look fancy and appear legitimate, but unbeknownst to you, it may contain critical errors or omissions that only become apparent after your death, leading to costly disputes, delays, or unintended outcomes. More importantly, a computer is not a human being. It cannot fully understand your unique family dynamics, the complexities of a blended family, the challenges of caring for a child with disabilities, or the emotional consequences these decisions may have in real life. It cannot anticipate the potential for conflict among loved ones, appreciate how an inheritance may affect each of your loved ones differently, or account for every legal nuance and intricacy that makes your family's circumstances unique.

I have a coffee cup on my desk that reads, "Please do not confuse your Google search with my law degree," and the same logic applies here. The internet is a terrible place to give yourself a medical diagnosis and it's just as bad when it comes to learning about the law because there is a lot of misinformation out there. Consider that AI platforms "learn" based on everything that has ever been written on the internet, and they are regurgitating a lot of that same information. In addition to that, when AI doesn't have an answer, it can hallucinate flawed information and present it as though it were accurate. All in all, we're not quite there yet when it comes to replacing lawyers with AI. At this stage, I wouldn't even trust it to do my legal research or document drafting without fact-checking and researching every source it cites, let alone entrust my family's future to information that may or may not be correct.

When it comes to estate planning, mistakes can result in costly and dire consequences for your family. Every state has very specific laws that must be followed exactly for a Will to be valid, and if one error is made in the process, then all your time and money will be wasted. So, if you are inclined to DIY your estate plan, please take the time and effort to educate yourself on ALL your options, EVERY document that you will need, and the specific legal requirements of your state to make sure your plan is valid.

The five fatal mistakes that I see people make most often when attempting to DIY their estate plans are:

1. They don't understand the complexities of estate planning or their options, and as a result, their plans are destined to fail from the start.
2. They don't sign their documents correctly.
3. They choose the wrong state forms or fill them out incorrectly.
4. They don't complete all the necessary documents that they need—including a Trust, a Will, Advance Medical Directives, Powers of Attorney, HIPPA waiver, or short-term and long-term Guardian Nominations for their children—or they do so incorrectly.
5. They do not inform their friends and family of the roles they were appointed to, how to implement their estate plan, or that the documents exist and where to find them.

THE TYPICAL ESTATE PLANNING EXPERIENCE

If you've met with a lawyer to complete your estate plan, congratulations! I commend you for being in the small percentage of the population that has done so. If you have, then you're probably aware that the traditional estate planning experience consists of spending one to three hours with an attorney. During the initial meeting, the clients spend a majority of the time schmoozing with the lawyer and answering a few basic questions about their wishes. The lawyer then tells them what plan they need, quotes their fee, and the client agrees to move forward and makes a payment. Within weeks, they meet for the second and final meeting to sign documents. They then take those home, put the binder on their office shelf, and feel relieved that they have completed the responsible task of estate planning and have protected their family.

Unfortunately, even when people take the time and make the investment of hiring a lawyer to help them create a plan, they can run into a lot of the same problems we identified with a DIY plan. A few of those issues are:

- **Lack of Experience:** The attorney may or may not specialize in estate planning. I have many friends who "do a little bit of estate planning work." They're typically real estate or family law attorneys who have an outdated form that was provided to them and a basic understanding of estate planning, but by no means are they experts and they typically have a one-size-fits-all approach. They charge much less, but with good reason, considering they are asking all their clients the same ten to fifteen questions, the conversation stays surface level, and for the most part, they're just quickly swapping your name into one of a few stock plans that they've "drafted" for everyone else. An experienced estate planning attorney will spend more time, meticulously discussing, designing, and drafting a customized and thorough estate plan for their clients.

- **Lack of Knowledge:** There are many estate planning lawyers who have been practicing for decades and provide a great service to their clients but have gotten comfortable doing things their way. Often referring to themselves as "old-school" or "old-fashioned," they like to discuss the good old days and what it was like before the age of the internet. But trust, probate, and tax laws are constantly changing and evolving. Those same lawyers admit they aren't as familiar with the latest technology, laws, IRS regulations, or developments in planning as they would like to be. Estate planning is a cutting-edge area of the law that changes quickly to keep up with the world we live in, and estate planning lawyers must stay on top of the latest trends to provide extraordinary service. Today, that means investing a small fortune each month on software and education. Only lawyers who specialize and focus on estate planning are making the necessary investments of time and money to stay current and provide their clients with the service they deserve.

- **Lack of Client Education:** Lawyers simply aren't spending enough time to get to know their clients and their family dynamics or to educate them on the many options that are available. As a result, people may not be aware that there is a better option for their specific circumstances, and in the end, they don't have the plan that would best suit their family.
- **Lack of Direction:** At the conclusion of most estate plan signings, you're typically provided with written instructions that describe what you need to do to properly implement your plan and when it is necessary to update your documents. The problem is that most lawyers don't explain that funding your trust and what you do after leaving their office is the most crucial part of the planning process. So, those funding instructions then sit neatly on your shelf, tucked away in your estate planning binder, and your family is the first to read them after they've sat for years collecting dust. Due to a lack of direction, education, or follow-through on your part, it's often too late to follow those instructions. I can't tell you how many of my clients, colleagues, friends, and family members have Trusts, but didn't realize they had to change the title of their house and the name on their accounts for their Trust to do what it was intended to do.
- **Lack of Follow Up:** Most lawyers charge by the hour. Others charge a flat fee. But they all charge you for their time. Years down the road, when you have a question about your estate plan and call to get an answer, you will

typically get a bill in the mail at the end of the month. As a result, most people avoid ever calling again. There isn't a system in place for periodic communication between the lawyer and client. So, as their life changes and they get married or divorced, have children, acquire or sell property, or move out of state, their plan does not change with them. In the end, their plan either fails or requires litigation, at a far greater expense than it would have cost to simply update it and manage their trust properly. Estate planning is not a "set it and forget it" exercise; it is a plan that must evolve with your life over time.

THE FAMILY, WEALTH & LEGACY PLAN

As you now know, estate planning is more than just drafting documents. That is why my firm doesn't use the term "estate plan," but instead refers to the documents we create as a Family, Wealth & Legacy Plan™. Our process is designed to be a family-centered solution for all your planning needs. Your life cannot be summed up in a balance sheet and there is far more to wealth than just money. Ensuring that your loved ones are well-taken care of and provided for, and that your family, wealth, and legacy will be protected, is as important as addressing your finances if a worse-case scenario becomes reality.

That is why it's imperative that you find an attorney who's willing to take the time to ensure that you understand what you're doing, why you're doing it, and what you need to do after walking out of their office. We pride ourselves on taking these steps in our planning process:

- **Education:** We take the time to get to know our clients and understand their goals, unique family dynamics, and the outcome they want, for not only their lives, but also for future generations of their family. Along the way, we spend some extra time educating them on life's most common legal problems and how to avoid them.
- **Custom Design:** We work with our clients to design a custom plan that serves their family's needs. We provide them with a variety of documents, systems, and options to not only ensure that their assets are protected, but to also guarantee that their values, life lessons, family history, and memories will pass to future generations of their family.
- **Implementation:** After completing their plan, we have systems in place to follow up with our clients to make certain they follow our instructions to properly implement it, and that their team of retirement, insurance, and tax advisers are all working together to effectuate the outcome.
- **Regular Revision:** We schedule an annual or three-year review to ensure that as each client's family grows and flourishes, their estate plan evolves along with them.
- **Execution:** Upon our client's death or incapacity, we work with their family to ensure their plan is carried out as intended. We help the family through their difficult

time so they can focus on what is most important. They aren't burdened with legal issues as we are there at every step to help them understand their loved one's plan and any actions that need to be taken, and to minimize unnecessary conflict during an emotional and stressful time.

As you can see, it is vital to work with an estate planning attorney who not only knows what they are doing, but who also takes the time and effort to ensure that you also understand your options, what you're signing, and what must be done to properly manage your assets and estate over time. It also doesn't hurt to find someone who genuinely cares about your family's well-being and has systems in place to keep in touch and maintain a long-term relationship.

We lawyers refer to estate planning as transactional law; clients enter into a one-time transaction with a lawyer where they exchange money for documents. But the traditional model of estate planning fails because of the process. Lawyers increase their profits by moving clients along the conveyor belt of estate planning as quickly as possible. As a result, the clients are not educated, and they do not understand their options, their plan, or how to update or implement it properly. They also don't take the time to consult and coordinate their advisers and loved ones during the estate planning process so they are all aligned and working together. It is an unfortunate reality, but most estate plans will fail under this transactional approach.

At our firm, we refer to estate planning as Family, Wealth & Legacy Planning because this process is so much more than a simple one-time transaction. Fundamentally, estate planning involves any form of preparation that you have done for your future. Whether you realize it or not, you've already put a team of people in place to help protect you in life and death. Your team is made up of your financial advisers, insurance advisers, tax advisers, real estate advisers, health care providers, and your kid's childcare provider, school, and babysitter. Anyone who is managing your wealth, assets, health, or kids is on your team. You're the coach who calls the plays, while your estate planning attorney draws them up for you. Your doctor, life insurance broker, and the people taking care of your kids are protecting you and playing defense, while the people managing your money are playing offense and looking to score. Estate planning lawyers can draw up whatever documents you ask us to, but unless you're actively participating and making sure that all the other players are in the right position and running in the right direction, all the strategizing and planning in the world is worthless.

For these reasons, we believe that estate planning is built on developing a lifelong relationship with our clients as their trusted adviser. We serve clients of every age and at every stage of life, but we especially love helping young families and developing a working relationship with their advisers over time. Estate planning not only requires strategic and intentional planning, but also ongoing coordination to ensure that your plan will succeed and put you in a position to win the game of life when time runs out. That is why we're happy to provide our clients with ongoing guidance and information on how to build their team, interview and select an adviser, invest their wealth, put the right insurance in place, and get their financial house in order.

CHAPTER 6

WHAT HAPPENS IF YOU BECOME INCAPACITATED?

Make the most of today. Time waits for no man. Yesterday is history. Tomorrow is a mystery. Today is a gift. That's why it is called the present.

—ALICE MORSE EARLE

Over the last seventy years, advancements in technology and medicine have increased our life expectancy by decades. People are living longer, and there is a significant increase in degenerative disease that comes along with age, like Alzheimer's and Parkinson's. And that's not to mention all the other risks and dangers that we face on a daily basis, regardless of how old you may be. We all know someone whose life was forever changed or ended too soon from a life-altering injury, disease, or debilitating medical issue.

It is imperative that you have the proper medical documents in place to not only save your life if something should ever happen to you, but also to protect your family from unnecessary attorney fees, court costs, delay, and possible conflict in a time of crisis. You may remember the case of Terri Schiavo, which was playing out around the time of OJ Simpson's first trial. Now, if you were too young, or simply don't recall the details… in 1990, at the age of twenty-six, alone at night in her kitchen, Ms. Schiavo unexpectedly went into cardiac arrest. By the time her husband found her on the kitchen floor and called for help, her brain had been deprived of oxygen, causing severe brain damage that left her in a permanent vegetative state.[22] For the next fifteen years, what was left of her life turned into a legal battle that played out in the national spotlight.[23] The simple version of the story is that after years of Ms. Schiavo being artificially kept alive, her husband wanted her suffering to end and directed the doctor to remove the artificial nutrition and hydration, but her family wanted her to remain on a feeding tube. This very personal and difficult decision led to Ms. Schiavo's family

---

22 Mayo Clinic. Christopher Hook and Paul Mueller. Volume 80, Issue 11, P1449-1460, November 2005. The Terri Schiavo Saga: The Making of a Tragedy and Lessons Learned. https://www.mayoclinicproceedings.org/article/S0025-6196%2811%2961439-0/fulltext.

23 Capote, Nick, dir. *Between Life & Death: Terri Schiavo's story.* 2023. https://www.imdb.com/title/tt27762075/.

and her husband suffering through fourteen appeals in Florida, five federal lawsuits, and four denials from the United States Supreme Court. It became global news and a worldwide debate, where the Vatican, the governor of Florida, Congress, and the president of the United States got involved. The saddest part of this cautionary tale is that fifteen years of pain and financial devastation could've easily been avoided if Ms. Schiavo's loved ones had simply known what she would have wanted or she had taken the time to complete a simple two-page form.

The takeaway is that our days are numbered. Your life and legacy will be dictated by the choices you make and by taking ownership over what you can control in life. As the Chinese proverb says, "The best time to plant a tree was twenty years ago. The second-best time is now."

Anyone over the age of eighteen should, at a minimum, have basic estate planning documents in place to record their wishes and appoint someone they trust to make financial and medical decisions for them, just in case an accident or illness leaves them unable to make their own choices. The names of these documents vary by state, but they include Powers of Attorney for Health Care, Health Care Proxy, Durable Power of Attorney, Advance Medical Directive, Living Will, and a HIPAA Waiver of Authorization.

The importance of these documents goes well beyond simply protecting your family from probate court. They can mean the difference between life and death in critical moments and permit doctors to access your medical records, medical history, allergies, blood type, and any other information that may be needed in an emergency to keep you alive. These documents will name who you want to make decisions on your behalf. They will provide your family and friends with your specific instructions, avoid unnecessary disagreement, and ease the burden of making extremely difficult decisions. Above all, they will serve as a guide in a time of great crisis. There will be no blame, resentment, or family conflict, as your family will rest assured knowing that they're simply following your wishes. Your family won't be forced to live out the rest of their days wondering whether they made the right choice or if it's what you would have wanted, because it was your decision, not theirs.

For instance, imagine that you and your spouse are in a catastrophic car accident and are fighting for your lives. Your entire family is at the hospital with your best friend and two children, who are eighteen and twenty. Your best friend has a medical background (doctor, nurse, or EMT) and they've known you your entire life. You've discussed your medical issues with them, gossiped, and swapped stories about what you do or do not want if anything should ever happen to you.

Are you aware that in those critical moments at the hospital, if you don't have these documents in place, your young, naive (and potentially irresponsible) children will be forced to make the final decision on your care or whether you'll be kept on life support? Even though they're only eighteen and twenty, they are adults and have the highest priority under the law. So instead of your best friend with a medical background who knows what you really wanted making the call, this decision will be the responsibility of your kids. Is that what you want if you have the choice?

More importantly, do your children know if you want to be kept alive artificially if there's no chance of recovery? Will they be able to agree on how to answer that question or will they feel guilty when faced with this difficult decision? If your children decide to keep you on life support, your family will now have to petition the court to have a guardian appointed on your behalf to access your bank accounts to pay your bills and manage your finances and health care. During that process, your children, your best friend, and your siblings may now be sitting on opposite sides of a courtroom, in conflict over who should be named guardian and have authority over your money and medical decisions. Their relationship may never be the same, and it could destroy any future relationship between your children, your family, and your best friend at a time when they need each other more than ever. If that's not enough to convince you, the fight in probate court will cost your family tens of thousands of dollars (if not more), all over an issue that could have been taken care of for a fraction of the cost if you had simply invested the time to have an estate plan prepared when you had the chance.

If, at the age of twenty-six, Terri Schiavo had known that her husband and parents would endure seven years of litigation and spend the entirety of their life savings arguing over the end of her life, do you think she would have taken the time to legally document her wishes?

These life-altering decisions can either destroy families or bring them together. Do not allow the final moments of your life to become a cautionary tale, but rather an example for your family because you cared enough to document your wishes and relieve them of the burden of having to make those difficult decisions for you.

This list outlines the bare minimum you need to know as an introduction to these advance directives:

- **HIPAA Waiver:** Your documents must expressly waive the privacy protections of a federal law known as HIPAA, and name specific people you've chosen who are allowed access to your private health information when you are unable to give permission.
- **Health Care Directives:** These documents provide your doctor and your family with specific instructions on how you want medical decisions to be made. They will include what life-saving measures and treatments you want to have taken to sustain your life artificially (Living Will or Advance Medical Directive). They will also allow you to choose who will make medical decisions for you, and name successors to serve as backups (Health Care Power of Attorney or Health Care Proxy). These documents will also express your instructions for mental health treatment, organ donation, and final arrangements for burial, cremation, etc. (Health Care Power of Attorney,

Declaration for Mental Health Treatment, Appointment of Agent to Control Disposition of Remains, and Remembrance and Services Memorandum).

These documents allow your family or friends to avoid probate if you lost the capacity to make decisions or care for yourself. They will appoint the people you want to make medical decisions for you, detail your instructions, and enable your loved ones to quickly access your medical records and bills to ensure they are paid, all without having to go to court.

When speaking to my clients, family, and friends, I also make sure to provide important warnings. If you've appointed someone to act as your Power of Attorney, Guardian, Representative, Trustee, etc.…you need to tell them. My recommendation is that you discuss your wishes with them and let them know where they can find your estate plan. When no one knows their role or where to find the documents in an emergency, it's as if they don't exist when you need them most. Furthermore, you want to make sure that they'll be capable of following your instructions, even if that means making a difficult decision.

If you didn't use an attorney, you need to make sure that the documents have been completed, signed, notarized, and witnessed properly. If one signature is missing, a mandatory line or decision is left blank, it may invalidate the entire document. I recommend bringing these documents to your primary care provider, reviewing them with your doctor, and having them saved in your file and in any health care portal associated with your provider(s). If your doctor's medical group has a specific form that they prefer to use, it's better to be aware of that and sign any necessary documents while you can. The same advice applies to supplying all of your financial documents to your financial adviser, bank, and anywhere else you have financial accounts. That way you can personally confirm that they are your documents, that they're valid, and that you're not missing any necessary legal language or documents that they'll require if emergency strikes.

Additionally, I typically don't recommend that you give the people you appoint in these roles a copy of the documents. Just tell them where your estate planning documents are in your home and make sure that they have the ability to access them when needed. That way, if you change your documents and update who you've appointed years down the road, they'll find the most recent, valid, and up-to-date version of your estate plan. The last thing you want is for two of your loved ones to be arguing in court over which document is valid and is your "real" plan, simply because there are too many old versions floating around.

However, one exception I'd make would be to give your loved ones a copy of your HIPPA waiver. If you haven't given your family or friends decision-making powers, I don't see any risk in providing them with the document because it merely provides them authorization to access your records. If you change your mind down the road and they happen to present an old copy to your doctor, what's the worst that can happen beyond them finding out how you're doing? But in an emergency, if your loved ones can't locate that waiver quickly or if it isn't on file with your providers, your doctors and hospital staff will not be able to freely communicate with them. They may not be able to receive updates or openly discuss your medical status when you are not able to communicate or advocate on your own behalf. Imagine what it would feel like if your eighteen-year-old child was injured at college several states away, and while they were unconscious in the ER, the hospital refused to speak with you (their parent) about their condition because they're an adult protected by HIPAA.

Advancements in technology have given us new tools to address these issues. Secure online vaults and cloud-based platforms can store your estate planning documents, advance directives, personal information, passwords, and instructions for your loved ones in one protected location. Many of these platforms also allow you to grant specific individuals secure access, so they can retrieve important information immediately when it is needed most.

When choosing a provider, look for one that offers strong security protections, including alerts whenever someone attempts to access your account or data. I also recommend using a reputable password manager. With proper planning, you can then document one master password and put it with your estate planning documents. That one password will then give your loved ones a simple and secure way to access all your financial, medical, and online accounts if something unexpected happens to you.

If you would like more information about these documents or the decisions that you need to make to complete them, please go to www.fwlls.com. If you live in Illinois and you'd like to chat with me directly, please do. If you live in one of the other 49 great states, please reach out for a referral, or consult with a qualified estate planning lawyer near you who can assist you in taking action to plan for your family.

CHAPTER 7

WHAT HAPPENS TO YOUR KIDS IF SOMETHING HAPPENS TO YOU?

The most important thing that parents can teach their children is how to get along without them.

—FRANK A. CLARK

There are only a few intrinsically significant motivations in life that move people to create an estate plan. A parent's innate instinct to protect their children and give them the best possible life is one of the most powerful motivations for investing the time and money necessary to create an estate plan.

It's natural for parents to want to provide their children with an extraordinary life, keep them safe, ensure they are loved, and give them the best possible opportunity to succeed. But no one is perfect, especially when it comes to raising kids. We all have moments that we regret and wish that we could take back. The question is, what example are you setting for your children now, and how will it influence their future?

The moment I found out my wife was pregnant, my brain went into overdrive. I obsessively began researching, ordered a dozen parenting books, and called my adviser to finally get the life insurance policy that I had put off getting for years as I started to prepare for what was to come. Then, when my daughter was born and I looked into those innocent, beautiful blue eyes, I suddenly realized that my primary job in life was to ensure that she was safe and well taken care of, no matter what. If you are a parent, you know what I am talking about. But the problem is that we don't know what we don't know, and unfortunately, parents of young children are statistically an unlikely demographic to think about planning for their potential demise or disability, while also being the most exposed and in need of planning.

As someone in his mid forties with little ones, I get it…parents with young kids are busy, sleep-deprived, overwhelmed, and just trying to keep the train on the tracks. Every day feels a little bit like Groundhog Day, with a tiny dictator demanding every second of your attention. You struggle to manage even the simplest of tasks while chasing a mini tornado around the house as it destroys everything in its path. So the thought of devoting time and money that you don't have toward estate planning is naturally the easiest thing to put on the backburner. However, if the worst-case scenario became your family's reality, it is undoubtedly the most important thing you can do to protect your family's future.

During my first estate planning meetings with parents, I make them face this reality head-on. One of the first things I ask is if they know what will happen to their children if they don't make it home from our meeting. Then, I sit back and watch their mental gymnastics play out as the weight of this question sinks in. As they realize that they have no clue what would happen and have never considered the legal ramifications of this important question, they typically go through the five stages of grief[24] right before my eyes. Others jump into justification mode, expecting that there has to be an acceptable answer and that somehow or some way, their family, the law, or life would ensure their kids would be taken care of.

If protecting your children is your motivation for estate planning, the goal is to ensure that they are cared for by the people you've chosen and that your assets are preserved and distributed responsibly, while avoiding unnecessary taxes, court costs, and attorney's fees. These goals are easy to attain. In a few hours, over a handful of meetings, you can achieve each one of them, and so much more, with a well-thought-out and customized estate plan.

---

24 Made famous by Dr. Elisabeth Kübler-Ross in her book *On Death and Dying*.

If you get your house in order now, while you still have the power to do so, it will prepare and organize your family for the future. The act of signing your documents and bringing your fancy binder home will provide you with peace of mind, confidence, certainty, and comfort in knowing that if the unimaginable should become reality for your family, your children's future will be protected.

Considering how eye-opening it is for my clients when they are forced to face the real-life consequences of what would happen in that scenario, I want to do a similar exercise with you. This will help ensure that you understand the importance of having a thorough and personalized estate plan. So, let's take a moment to face the harsh realities of what could happen if you and your spouse don't make it home and don't have a plan in place.

FOSTER CARE

Imagine you and your spouse are in a car accident on your way home from an evening out. After hours of leaving unanswered voicemails, the babysitter begins to panic and calls the police (like any good babysitter would). When the police arrive, they tell your sitter that you've been in an accident, you're unconscious, in critical condition, and that your spouse is in life-saving surgery. They ask the sitter for your relative's contact information because the sitter does not have legal authority to continue caring for your children. No matter how well the sitter knows them, or how much they plead to stay, the police simply cannot leave your children in the sitter's care. Until the police can find a family member (your next of kin), or someone with documented legal authority, your children will need to be turned over to child protective services. They may then be forced to face the reality that you've been seriously injured, or even killed, while surrounded by strangers in foster care.

Even if your best friends and neighbors saw all the commotion as the police arrived and came over to demand that the children stay with them, the police are legally required to place your children with child protective services until someone who has the authority to care for them shows up or is appointed by a court order. If your family lives close by and the authorities can get in touch with them quickly, your children may only spend a short amount of time in the care of the police or social services. But if your family lives halfway across the country, or if the guardians you chose in your Will are on vacation, it may take days before someone your children know and trust can get to them. Plus, your named guardians will only be discovered if people know where to find your estate planning documents and can quickly provide them to the police.

Two examples of this have stuck with me over the years. In one case, a woman dropped her two small children off at a one-hour class and decided to use the time to go to the gym. While exercising on the treadmill, she went into cardiac arrest and died from an undetected heart condition. Her husband was away on business in Europe. While he was frantically trying to catch a flight home, his kids were placed in the care of the police and social services. The second instance involved a woman who was T-boned by a semi-truck while driving to pick up her son from kindergarten. Authorities notified the school, who then contacted her husband, a truck driver who was halfway across the country at the time. The man quickly gave the school authority to release his son to the family's neighbor, who was listed as the boy's registered backup emergency contact for the school. However, the police picked up the child from the neighbor's house and placed him into the custody of social services until the boy's father returned home. Only the relatives of a child have legal authority to care for them, so in both instances, when no immediate family members were able to step in quickly, social services had to.

Whether it's hours or days that your children spend in the care of the police, social services, child protective services, or foster care, any amount of time is too long. As a parent, it is within your power to prevent this from ever becoming a possibility if you have an emergency plan in place with a few simple legal documents.

Your emergency plan can also prevent the possibility of your family, friends, or loved ones having to go to court to appoint a temporary legal guardian for your children. But if you don't have the proper legal documents in place and your children are temporarily placed with a family member, whoever is then willing to step up to take on the role of your children's guardian will have to retain an attorney, file a legal case, and spend thousands of dollars and the next few months in court to be formally appointed—all while they are mourning your serious injury or death and consoling and caring for your children. If more than one person thinks they are best suited to care for your kids, then a legal battle may play out in a courtroom for months, if not years. In the end, any time that is spent in court will cost your family much more than the money you would have spent on an estate plan, and you will no longer have any input or control over who will raise your children.

WHO WILL RAISE YOUR CHILDREN?

Selecting guardians for your children is an extremely difficult decision for most parents and one that often prevents couples from completing their estate plan. You and your spouse could spend years debating who to name as guardians because naturally, no one can replace you or care for your kids as well as you do. But let me be clear, ***any choice you make is better than not making a choice at all***. Your gut reaction is usually the right one, and if your choice isn't sitting well with you in a few years, you can always update your documents. It is a simple change and shouldn't cost much money. However, your failure to plan and simply make a choice could be devastating to your children's future and cause conflict between your family and friends at a time when they should be rallying around and supporting your children.

Important note: The likelihood of something happening to both you and your spouse is statistically so remote that I view this decision as merely a responsible and necessary form of insurance. Similarly, it's statistically very unlikely that a tornado will suck up my house like something out of the *Wizard of Oz*, and as a result, I'm not going to lose sleep over the possibility.

Instead, I will do the responsible thing, choose an insurance company I feel I can trust to protect my family and our financial wealth, and go on with my day.

Whatever you do, please don't let the never-ending guardian debate prevent you from moving forward. You can always change your named guardians as your life evolves, and that's why it's important to review your plan every few years. But the last thing you want to do is leave this important decision up to the court system, or even worse, force your family and friends into a long, expensive legal battle over your kids.

THE CHILDREN'S PROTECTION PLAN

A traditional estate planning experience will name guardians for your children as well as a backup set of guardians just in case. Yet, as a parent, there is so much more that needs to be considered and implemented when designing your plan, which is often overlooked in the typical estate planning experience. Think about what you would do if you left your kids to take a weekend trip. You wouldn't merely pick a babysitter and hope everything turned out okay. You'd probably give them a tour of the house, a twenty-minute speech, a manual of instructions, and call to check in on them multiple times a day. Yet, sadly, in the document that will provide your final set of parenting instructions, you're often providing far less guidance, if any, on how you want your children to be cared for than you do for the weekend babysitter.

At our firm, we specialize in helping young families protect what is most important. That is why we have developed the Children's Protection Plan™, which is one component of the Family, Wealth & Legacy Planning Process™. The Children's Protection Plan was designed to address areas where the traditional estate planning experience falls short.

Depending on which attorney you choose, the typical estate planning process consists of one to two hours of face time in an initial meeting to design your plan. It's simply not enough time to get know you, your wishes, and your family dynamics, and help you work through these very important decisions. More guidance, education, and planning is necessary to ensure that parents understand the importance of having a detailed emergency plan in place for their children and how to properly implement that plan once they leave the attorney's office.

To guarantee that your children's well-being is going to be protected, you need to understand a few key concepts: (1) the importance of naming both long-term and short-term guardians for your children, (2) which instructions to provide your children's babysitters and childcare providers, and (3) what guidance you need to leave behind for your children's guardians.

SHORT-TERM GUARDIANS

I'm sure you have neighbors, friends, or family living close by who know and love your children. You may not have chosen them to raise your kids or to be their long-term guardian, but you would be extremely grateful to know that they were there to comfort and care for your children in the event of an emergency. Part of our process includes assisting our clients in the selection of short-term guardians and ensuring that in the event of an emergency, our client's plans play out seamlessly. An emergency plan is essential because if the long-term guardians you've chosen are unavailable, on vacation, or don't live close by, you have built a system of checks and balances to ensure your children's safety in times of uncertainty, so they are NEVER placed in foster care (or with your bitchy sister, alcoholic brother, or narcissistic parent[25]—pick your poison; every family has its issues).

Depending on what state you live in, you may be able to legally appoint someone as a short-term guardian for your children. In Illinois, you can grant someone legal authority to care for your children for up to one year.[26] Within the Appointment of Short-Term Guardian form for Illinois, you can choose from twelve different options to define the specific circumstances under which someone has a legal right to care for your kids. During our planning process, we always give our clients a blank copy of this form that has been signed and notarized so they have the flexibility to complete this important document whenever it may be needed. If the kids are going to Grandma's for a week or on vacation with their best friend, parents can quickly fill out

25 For the record, I do not have a sister, my brother is not an alcoholic, and my parents are wonderful, but after several rounds of editing and debate over the use of a particular word, and questionable labels for a family member that may be offensive, at the demand of my wonderful paralegal, we have elected to leave this as originally written because she thinks that it is extremely relatable in most households.

26 755 ILCS 5/11-5.4.

the form to give a responsible adult legal authority to care for the kids and (God forbid) make medical decisions in the event of an emergency. On the other hand, you can also authorize your best friends and neighbors to care for the kids until your siblings, or whomever you've chosen as permanent and long-term guardians, can travel from out-of-state to get to them.

LONG-TERM GUARDIANS

One of the most disappointing things we come across in the world of estate planning is when people invest the time and money to create a plan to protect their family, but it fails when they need it most. For example, in the traditional estate planning experience, people are simply instructed to choose guardians, and they usually select a couple: their parents, siblings, or best friend. But years go by, and the couple they selected may move, get divorced, or one of them may pass away. In those cases, there is no backup selected, or maybe you wouldn't have chosen your sibling or best friend if you knew they were going to be single when they were given custody of your kids. Even worse, what if you name your sibling and their spouse, but your sibling dies in the accident with you and now their spouse (who you aren't the biggest fan of) is now the single parent of your children? In the end, your plan has failed, and you don't get the result you would have wanted for your children.

When designing a Family, Wealth & Legacy Plan, we guide our clients through a proven process consisting of questionnaires and meetings to help them identify a list of potential long-term guardians, conditions for each of the guardians selected, and a succession plan. While going through these exercises, some of the conditions we've seen our clients incorporate most often are that the people they've chosen as guardians must be married, serve jointly as a couple, live in a particular state or city, attend a certain church, and facilitate time with family members.

We also have our clients identify whether there are any family members that they absolutely would never want to have raise their children, and we help them document why those people should be excluded from consideration. This "exclusion letter" will remain private and confidential, meaning no one will ever see it or even know it exists unless it absolutely needs to be used in court to challenge their petition for guardianship.

When going through our process to select guardians, our clients are asked to consider who they want their children to become ten, twenty, or thirty years in the future. We ask a series of questions, similar to the exercise you completed in Chapter 1, so we can shift a couple's focus from debating a list of individuals to a deeper conversation centered around who is best suited to guide and assist their children to attain the future they envision for them.

During this process, and when narrowing down their choices, we ask our clients to consider what is truly most important for them when it comes to raising their children:

- Geography (location and where they want their children to be raised)
- Two-parent household (Marital Status)

- Proximity to extended family
- Willingness to facilitate a relationship with family
- Values
- Maturity, temperament, & patience
- Time available
- Discipline & parenting style
- Demeanor
- Interests
- Financial ability
- Ability to travel
- Experiences that you want for your children
- Education
- Religion or spirituality
- Lifestyle
- Culture
- Language(s) spoken
- Political views
- Health
- Age & stamina

By the end of this process, clients have designed the future that they want for their children. As they have worked through this exercise, they've also created a list of instructions for their children's caregivers that outlines the experiences, activities, values, and character traits that are most important to them. This exercise works for two reasons: (1) it helps our clients make a very difficult decision while focusing on the outcomes they want for their kids, instead of merely arguing over a list of names, and (2) they are creating and documenting the instructions and guidance that they want to provide to their children's guardians and potentially the court. This way, not only have the parents carefully selected guardians for their children, but also, and more importantly, their instructions will help their chosen guardians truly know how they would have wanted the kids to be raised and their inheritance to be managed. There is no need for a legal hearing that will bypass their input.

Going through this process also helps our clients focus on how to be more present with their children amid the chaos that is parenting. It is our hope and goal that we can help our clients begin to consider what values, wisdom, and experiences they wish to impart to their children during the daily grind. Rather than always rushing to the next "thing" and shuttling the kids from place to place, dinners and downtime can become an opportunity for parents to teach their kids the life lessons, stories, traditions, and family history that they want to instill in them.

BABYSITTERS

A babysitter or nanny who is not a relative **does not** have legal authority to care for your kids. If an emergency strikes and they contact the police, regardless of how well they know your kids, how much they love them, and how willing they are to stay with them during an emergency, the police will be required to locate a relative to assume temporary custody of your children until it can be sorted out by the court. If they can't find a relative and the babysitter doesn't have their information, the police will have no choice but to turn your children over to child protective services until they can find someone legally authorized to care for your kids. That is why we create a fridge magnet for our clients listing their emergency contacts and short-term guardians, so in the event of an emergency, someone with legal authority to care for them will be contacted right away.

Our clients know to instruct their babysitters to:

Step 1: Go to the magnet on the fridge.

Step 2: Blow up the phones of everyone on that list until they reach someone who has the legal authority to care for the kids.

Step 3: Wait until after that person has arrived to call the authorities.

After completing the plan, we also send letters to each of the chosen guardians, providing them with the legal document they'll need and instructions on what to do in the event of an emergency. Naturally, no parent wants their children in foster care, and as you can see, it is extremely important to have a system of strategies, instructions, and contingency plans in place to ensure that will never happen.

If you'd like more information regarding the selection of guardians for your children, or to check out our downloadable resources, please visit: www.fwlls.com.

CHAPTER 8

WHAT HAPPENS TO YOUR MONEY AND ASSETS WHEN YOU DIE?

A good man leaves an inheritance to his children's children.

—PROVERBS 13:22

This book is intended to be an introduction. My goal is not to overwhelm or confuse you with overly complex financial strategies or estate planning options. Those subjects would require me to write volumes and are not something you should be thinking about until you complete your foundational estate plan (and are swimming in a pool full of gold coins like

Scrooge McDuck). Just like building a house, you need to lay the foundation before building the second story and a guest house. So, for now, we're merely going to focus on the basics, allowing you to get your ducks in a row and take the necessary precautions to avoid some of the most common difficulties that arise in everyday life. When it comes to your finances, the starting point must be getting organized and prepared, just in case anything should happen to you or your spouse.

With that in mind, let's imagine that your spouse survived that fateful car accident, and was left to raise your children on their own without an estate plan.

MANAGING FINANCES

In most marriages, one person typically assumes the chief financial officer (CFO) role and pays all the bills and manages the money. If you are the CFO in your relationship and something happens to you, your spouse may spend the weeks after your death rifling through filing cabinets, on the phone with account providers, and struggling to retrieve passwords, gain access to financial accounts, and track down your money. They must do this all while also trying to grieve, console your children, and make funeral arrangements. Financial disruption or stress over money, on top of an already tragic and devastating situation, is the last thing your loved ones need.

Legally, they may need to hire an attorney and go to court to gain access to any accounts their name wasn't directly on, but that only applies to the accounts they can find. What if they don't know about a particular account, or that you managed an investment account through an app on your phone? What if they don't know the passcode to your phone, or the password to your email? What if your spouse sells the house, moves, and deactivates your cell phone? Obviously, the bank or company wouldn't have a way to contact you, they wouldn't know you've died, and no one in your family would even know the account exists. Just so you are aware, after three years, the company will turn your money over to the state treasurer as "unclaimed property." Lawyers refer to this as property "escheating" to the state, but simply put, when a company holds money on your behalf, if they can't locate you for three years, they must turn it over to the state. In this fast-moving digital age, banks are now changing their policies to monitor whether you've logged into your account within the last three years. If you haven't, they send a letter, and if you don't answer it, your money will be turned over to your state treasurer.

This recently happened to me. Ten years ago, I took out an auto loan and in order to open my account, I was required to start a savings account with a minimum balance of a few hundred dollars. After I paid off the loan, I just left the money in the account and thought nothing of it. Recently, I got a letter alerting me that the $300 in my savings account was going to be turned over to the Department of Unclaimed Property within thirty days if I didn't respond. When I called in to ask why, the woman told me it's their policy to close the account and turn the money over to the state if you don't sign into your account for three years, despite the fact that they had all my contact information and I was still getting monthly statements mailed to me. It appears that your online activity is now the benchmark that companies are measuring above all else, even if you're not interacting with them online.

Nationally, states are holding over $70 billion in "unclaimed property."[27] Illinois is currently holding more than $5 billion[28] from situations exactly like this. It's shocking! Go look up what your state treasurer is currently holding, and while you're at it, run a search to see if you or a family member have a claim. It's estimated that one in seven Americans do, and that the average amount of all claims is $2,080. Through a simple national search, I discovered that two states were holding money that belonged to me—a paycheck and refunded fees from the Bureau of Motor Vehicles and county where I lived when I was in school decades ago.[29] I am alive, well, and responsible, and I had three small claims. If my accounts are being closed and claims already exist in my name while everything is great, I can't imagine what would happen to my wife if she was forced to track down everything I own without any guidance.

When it comes to money, the death of a family member (especially a spouse) has a ripple effect. Families often don't discuss finances in great detail, and the burden of paying the bills and managing the money typically falls to one person in a

27 National Association of Unclaimed Property Administrators (2025). unclaimed.org/.

28 Illinois State Treasurer (2025), *History*. icash.illinoistreasurer.gov/.

29 Missing Money (2025). http://www.missingmoney.com/.

marriage. If you don't have a plan and your family isn't financially organized, your spouse (or children) may spend months in crisis mode if something happens. That's why it's so important for you to take the simple step of safely tracking all your assets, accounts, and financial information in one place for your family to find if emergency strikes.

In our office, we provide every family with a financial inventory of all their assets and a simple system to implement that will ensure all their family's important accounts, passwords, death beneficiaries, and information are readily available when their family needs them the most. It takes our clients an hour or so up front to gather all the information, and with our system, no more than thirty minutes a year to keep it updated. It's not rocket science; it's a simple spreadsheet that tracks and totals all their assets. Anyone can create one, whether it's on paper, typed out, or in a basic Excel document. The point is that making a small investment of time to prepare and organize your finances will allow your family to quickly and easily identify all of your financial accounts, allowing them to focus on what is most important at a time when they simply want to grieve. If you want to go above and beyond, we always recommend that our clients document their username and passwords for all their important online accounts. It will make things much easier for your loved ones to access and get control over your estate and manage your digital footprint.

Bonus Tip: Every January, review your financial inventory and update each account balance so you can track how your finances have changed from year to year and how well your investments are performing in comparison to the overall market. While you're at it, double check if your accounts are properly titled in the name of your trust, and that all your beneficiary designations are up to date. If it were me, I would print a copy of my beneficiary designations to confirm they were updated and put them in my estate planning binder, just in case.

You should also verify that your usernames, passwords and account information are documented correctly and accessible. Better yet, use a reputable password manager and leave clear instructions with your estate planning documents explaining how your loved ones can access your accounts in an emergency.

DISTRIBUTION OF YOUR ESTATE

In Illinois, if you don't have an estate plan that says otherwise, the rules for "descent and distribution" require that all of your probate assets are divided, with 50 percent going to your spouse and 50 percent to your children.[30] Take a moment and think about that: If your spouse is sixty-five and trying to retire comfortably, your kids, who are in their thirties and don't need your money, will get half. Alternatively, if your children are toddlers, they still get half when your spouse needs that money to raise them without you.

So, the real-life application of the law requires your assets to be divided, regardless of your spouse or children's age, income, or

30 755 ILCS 5/2-1(a).

needs. This division forfeits several tax benefits for your family, offers less protection, and exposes them to more risk of losing their inheritance. If your kids are minors, your spouse may even get stuck paying for a bond and attorney's fees to file accountings with the court to justify how they're spending your kids' money every year. Shockingly, the court may even require that the money be frozen and made inaccessible unless your children's guardian hires an attorney to go to court and asks for permission every time they want a distribution. If this doesn't sound like the result you want for your family, the only way to avoid it is to get your estate plan in place and make your own decisions on how you want your property to be divided.

Remember, this only applies to assets that were solely titled in your name and must go through probate before being distributed to your family. Anything that is owned jointly will automatically pass to the joint owner, and any accounts or assets with a named beneficiary will automatically pass to them. Additionally, please keep in mind that the law is different in every state, and each county will handle things in their own unique way. I would recommend that unless you have the desire to research the law in your state, you consult with a professional in your county so you know if the government's default plan where you live is something you are okay with or need to address.

REMARRIAGE

Although it may be difficult for you to envision, let's imagine that, years after your death, your spouse remarries. Their new husband or wife has children from a prior marriage. Ten years into the marriage, your former spouse dies without an estate plan. All the joint bank accounts, the house, and anything else that they owned jointly automatically goes to their second spouse and your children receive nothing. Any accounts or assets that are titled only in your spouse's name will need to go through probate, and during the court process, those assets will be divided, with 50 percent going to their new spouse and 50 percent going to your children.

Let's imagine what that might look like.

Remarried Spouse's Estate			Who Would Inherit Your Spouse's Estate	
Asset	**Ownership**	**Value**	**New Spouse**	**Your Kids**
House	Owned Jointly	$500,000	$500,000	$0
Bank Accounts	Owned Jointly	$100,000	$100,000	$0
Life Insurance	Second Spouse & Kids (50/50)	$150,000	$75,000	$75,000
Retirement Accounts	Second Spouse & Kids (50/50)	$250,000	$125,000	$125,000
	Total Estate Value	**$1,000,000**	**$800,000**	**$200,000**

So, your spouse's second husband/wife will effectively inherit a majority, if not the entirety, of your life savings. Years later, when they pass away, everything will then legally go to their children or next of kin, and your children will receive nothing from their estate. Remember, this is exactly what happened to my mother and aunts when my grandmother passed, so please let that sink in, because it is more common than you would think. I can't tell you how many of my clients have told me that the exact same thing happened to someone in their family.

WHO WILL MANAGE YOUR MONEY?

Now, what happens in a scenario where both you and your spouse die in the accident, leaving your two young children behind without an estate plan in place?

After the court declares a member of your family the kids' legal guardian, the judge will also decide who will manage your life savings. The court may appoint a guardian of your children and a guardian of your estate (your assets); in other words, someone who will be the day-to-day parent and someone who will manage their money (the financial parent). Sometimes, the court gives both powers to the same person, and sometimes they don't. It's important to know that, when choosing guardians and creating a Will, it needs to instruct the court on who you've appointed to serve in both roles and waive the need to have a bond.

Regardless of whether the judge or your Will appoints them, the law requires the guardian of your estate (the financial parent) to obtain a bond at their own expense. The bond serves as an insurance policy to protect the money left behind for your children. This may sound like a good thing, but in real-life application it's another hoop to jump through in a time of crisis and will cost your family or friends money when they're volunteering to help your kids. Thankfully, the bond requirement is voluntary, and you can opt out of it in your Will.

If your Will doesn't waive this requirement, the guardian's credit score will determine if they qualify for the bond. If they qualify, meet the state's requirements, and are appointed, they will be required to account for every dollar that is spent of your money until your children turn eighteen. If they don't qualify and no one else who is eligible steps up and volunteers, the court may appoint a public guardian to manage your children's money. If this happens, the public guardian will charge fees for their time, and a stranger who does not know you or your children will then be in charge of deciding what is, and what is not, appropriate to pay for on your children's behalf.

For instance, let's imagine you had a basic form Will that simply named your sister as your children's guardian. But like most Wills, it named a guardian generally and didn't separate these roles to specifically name someone as the guardian of their person (day-to-day parent) and guardian of their estate (financial parent). So the court assumed you intended to appoint your sister in both roles. If she has bad credit and can't get a bond, or if she got arrested decades ago for something that the judge doesn't like, the court won't allow her to manage your money or make financial decisions for your kids. Instead, the court may appoint a public guardian. Even if your sister knows it was important to you that your children travel, play a musical instrument, attend private school, get tutoring, see a certain counselor after your death, or that you would have wanted her to get a bigger house to comfortably raise them, she will have to get approval from the public guardian because you didn't leave any instructions behind. As a result, these decisions will be left up to the judgment of a stranger, and if they don't think certain expenses, activities, or luxuries are reasonable, they will refuse to reimburse your sister. The public guardian is required by law to manage your children's inheritance frugally and prudently, so they will err on the side of caution. They will do all of this while charging your estate for their time and drawing from your life savings to do so.

WHEN WILL YOUR CHILDREN RECEIVE YOUR MONEY?

Unless specifically documented in a Trust, upon your children attaining the age of eighteen, they will receive the entirety of your estate. Take a moment and let that sink in. Are you okay with knowing that if something happened to you and your spouse, your eighteen-year-old would receive your life savings outright and be free to manage every dime of your money as they please? Put yourself in their shoes…if you received a large sum of money at the age of eighteen, would you have managed those funds responsibly? Would you have been motivated to go to college and work hard to pursue your education and a meaningful career? Would you have listened to, or respected, your guardian at the age of seventeen, when you knew that you had a large sum of money coming your way in a short period of time?

How much your children inherit will also be included in public court records for everyone to see. As a result, they may be targeted by predators and con artists. Once your kids get their checks, it will be their money outright, with no oversight or protection. So, the entirety of your life savings can be at risk or even lost to creditors, predators, lawsuits, or divorce.

Regardless of their age, if your kid decides to spend your money on a fancy new sports car and gets in an accident, the entirety of your wealth can be lost in a lawsuit. If your child gets married and puts your money into an account with their new spouse or adds their spouse's name to the title to your house, it will likely become "marital property," and if they get divorced, your life savings will be split with their ex.

Statistics show that one-third of all people who receive an inheritance spend, lose, or donate all of it, and actually end up with "negative savings."[31] In fact, over longer periods of

---

31 Zagorsky JL (2012). Do people save or spend their inheritances? Understanding what happens to inherited wealth. Journal of Family and Economic Issues; DOI 10.1007/s10834-012-9299-y.

"Many people who received an inheritance did not have positive savings even with the gift. Overall, more than one-third (34.9%) of all inheritors saw a decline or no change in their wealth after getting an inheritance."

"Bequests and inheritances are often windfalls. An individual has primarily two choices with a windfall: money can be saved or spent….Inheritances have similar characteristics to lottery prizes (Clotfelter and Cook 1990) since both give unearned windfalls to recipients. Research shows lottery winners saved just 16 cents of every dollar won (Imbens et al. 2001), bankruptcy rates soared for lottery winners 3–5 years after winning (Hankins et al. 2009) and college gamblers had more problematic financial behaviors than non-gamblers (Worthy et al. 2010). These facts suggest many people quickly spent windfalls. However, lottery winners likely have lower savings rates than inheritors because some inheritors expect to receive money, even if the exact timing, amount, and conditions are unknown or are surrounded by uncertainty."

time, on average only half of all inheritances are saved. This is because people typically view an inheritance as free money and a windfall. As a result, they spend their inheritance on luxuries, pay down debt, or aggressively invest for growth. When people come into a large sum of money, it's important that they have the experience and ability to manage it wisely. That's why it's critical to create a plan that thoughtfully spells out when your children will receive their inheritance and how they will receive it.

THE ASSET PROTECTION PLAN

The traditional estate planning experience may address some of these common issues, but based on our experience, not enough time is spent educating clients on the law, the options available to them, or what must be considered when designing their plan. During the Family, Wealth & Legacy Planning Process, we believe it is important to provide guidance and assist our clients to make several important financial decisions and ensure they understand the implications of those decisions. To do so, we take the necessary time and effort to review the following issues with them.

Selecting Financial Guardians

In most cases, our clients have a family member, friend, or trusted professional who they would have confidence in to handle their money but wouldn't choose to raise their children. When designing a Family, Wealth & Legacy Plan and selecting guardians, we help our clients evaluate their options and determine if they would prefer to appoint a financial guardian to oversee the management of their estate along with a guardian to care for their children. During this process, detailed instructions and guidance are created that will be provided to their children's guardians to confirm how they would want their children to be raised and how they would like them to be financially supported.

In our experience, most parents feel more comfortable with the idea of putting a system of checks and balances in place to better protect their children's financial future. Naturally, if a trusted family member, friend, or professional is in control of distributing your children's money in coordination with the guardian who will be caring for them day-to-day, there is more oversight and less opportunity for abuse or inappropriate spending. Your family and friends can work together to prudently manage your money in the manner that you have outlined to guide them. They can support your children's needs and lean on each other to give them the upbringing and experiences that you would have wanted for them, without the cost, oversight, or red tape of the probate court.

There are many important things for you to consider when selecting financial guardians, but here are the five suggestions we use to guide our clients.

Qualifications: Are they qualified to manage your life savings? They don't have to be a financial adviser or an accountant, but they do need to be organized and responsible enough to fulfill their legal duties, keep good records, make sure things are done on time, and work with a professional to address financial and tax issues. You can even document who you'd like (or require) them to work with if you have a trusted adviser or accountant you'd prefer.

Guidance: Document how you would like your estate to be managed if you have any preferences. For instance, you can document if you want the guardians to give your children money whenever they want (liberally),[32] only when certain conditions are met and if they really need it (conservatively),[33] or you can specify certain incentives when a distribution will be made, such as graduation from college, birth of a child, starting a business, or when they buy their first home.

---

32 The standard language that is commonly provided in a Trust when you choose to provide your beneficiaries with liberal distribution guidelines is: "In making discretionary distributions to [beneficiaries' names], I desire to provide for their well-being and happiness. Although I request that my Trustee consider the other known resources available to [beneficiaries names] before making distributions, I also request that my Trustee be liberal in making any distributions to, or for their benefit. I acknowledge that the principal of the trust established for [beneficiaries names] may be exhausted in making these distributions."

33 The standard language that is commonly provided in a Trust when you choose to provide your beneficiaries with conservative distribution guidelines is: "In making discretionary distributions to the beneficiary, it is my desire that the beneficiary develops a strong work ethic, be a productive and contributing member of society, and provide for those who are dependent on the beneficiary for care and support. Accordingly, my Trustee shall be mindful of, and always take into consideration, the other known resources available to the beneficiary before making discretionary distributions. It is my desire that preservation of principal be a priority for purposes of this trust share and that genuine need be shown by the beneficiary before my Trustee makes any discretionary distribution."

If you have any particular views on investing, you can document how you'd like your money to be managed and whether you support a conservative investment approach, growth-oriented, ESG, gold, silver, real estate, or holding cryptocurrency. Some of these investments are not permitted under the prudent investor rule, and if you own risky investments when you die, they will need to be sold if your wishes aren't documented. In addition, it can be extremely valuable to provide guidance and written instructions on what you do and do not want your children's inheritance to be spent on.

Time and Ability: Are they willing to take on this responsibility, and do they have the time and ability? They should be organized, responsible, and capable of managing your estate. It will take time and it's a big responsibility, so we recommend that our clients document that their financial guardians can be paid for their time, and if they want, they can even choose an appropriate hourly amount.

Working Relationship: The guardians you choose to manage your money and raise your kids need to have a good working relationship and the ability to cooperate in your children's best interests. In my opinion, this is the most important factor to consider, as long as they're also organized and will keep good records.

Backup Nominations: Select as many potential backups (successors) as you can think of in case the guardian is unable to serve or needs to resign from their role. After your family and friends, you should consider naming advisers and professionals you know, like, and trust, so they are listed as options and your list is as long as possible. It's better to have a long list of people you know and trust as opposed to having a stranger appointed. Correspondingly, you may want to consider naming a professional to serve with your family and friends to remove emotion and to act as a check and balance because they will be objective and have the expertise to do the job. An experienced estate planning attorney can help introduce you to some reputable Trust Officers and professional corporate trustees in your local area.

Choosing When Your Children Will Receive Their Inheritance

Do you believe it is a good idea for your children to receive the entirety of your life savings at the age of eighteen? I've never met a parent who believes this is an ideal solution. If you want to avoid this result, the ONLY way is through a Trust. **If you have a Will or no plan at all, your children will receive your life savings at eighteen.** This is one of the main reasons I believe that all parents should have a Trust in place. It offers parents the option to choose what they believe is best for their family as opposed to state law dictating it. You can select certain ages that your children will receive their inheritance, you can choose milestones where they receive distributions, or you can elect to keep the money protected in a Trust indefinitely.

These decisions are very personal and different for every family. You will need to take many considerations into account, including your child(ren)'s age, maturity, level of responsibility, whether they have any disabilities, any issues with drugs, alcohol, or gambling, a rocky marriage, and your own personal views on wise financial management. When assisting clients, the choices we most commonly see are:

- **Outright Distribution:** All the money is distributed when the children reach a particular age (twenty-five, thirty, thirty-five, forty).
- **Staggered Distributions (Ages & Stages):** The money is distributed at various ages (twenty-five, thirty, thirty-five) or defined increments of time following your death (such as five, ten, or fifteen years). These distributions can be spread out however you wish, either in thirds, or in any combination of percentages (25 percent, 25 percent, and the remaining 50 percent).
- **Annual Distributions:** You can give them the option of taking specific amounts or percentages of the total value of the assets held by the Trust annually. The most common distribution is a "Five by Five Power," where the beneficiary is entitled to receive either $5,000 or 5 percent of the Trust principal each year, whichever is greater.
- **Discretionary Distributions:** You can give your children's trustee broad discretion to decide when to provide your children with a payment from the Trust, or limit their authority based upon ascertainable legal standards such as health, education, maintenance, or support. In addition, you can provide guidance to the trustee to make distributions for certain milestones or achievements,

or set requirements to be met for your kids to receive distributions (known as incentive provisions). The most common are gifts for college tuition, graduation, starting a business, marriage, the purchase of a home, birth of a child, etc.

- **Asset Protection (General Needs) Trust:** Your estate remains in separate Trusts for your children indefinitely, where their trustee can provide them with discretionary distributions.

ASSET PROTECTION

If you are concerned with asset protection, you can give your children and future generations of your family a lifelong gift that will provide an example of responsible wealth management. If you choose to leave your children's inheritance to them in a "General Needs Trust," upon your death, your estate will continue to be held in trust for your kids pursuant to your instructions. By doing so, you can choose from a multitude of options, some of which can minimize estate taxes and preserve your family's wealth for generations by shielding their inheritance from lawsuits, creditors, and divorce.

If you choose to leave your children's inheritance to them in trust and not to give them control after they turn eighteen, the first decision you will need to make is when your children's "shares" of the estate will be created. Their shares can be created immediately, or you can require your estate be held in a "Common Pot" Trust, either indefinitely or until your youngest child reaches a certain age. The most typical reason for creating a Common Pot Trust is to allow all the kids to graduate from college before the money is divvied up between them and their shares of the estate are created. The logic is that if you've paid for one of your kids to get through college and you passed away before your youngest graduated from high school, it would put them at a disadvantage and it wouldn't be fair if they had to pay for college out of their share. If you're interested in keeping your estate in a Common Pot Trust indefinitely, there usually needs to be a reason, and you can get into some complicated structures that often become what are referred to as "Dynasty Trusts." For most families, however, this isn't necessary and the focus is simply on whether they would feel more comfortable with a Common Pot Trust until their youngest graduates from college.

Once shares are created, they will be divided into separate General Needs Trusts for each child. Each Trust will get its own federal tax ID and become an entity in the eyes of the government. The trustee will be required to file a tax return and keep records and accountings, just like a corporation, but in this case, the only purpose of the entity (or your families corporation) is to hold and manage your children's inheritance on their behalf. Depending on which option you select, it is up to you how long these Trusts will remain in effect and when your kids are entitled to receive their inheritance outright, free and clear. If you are interested in providing your kids with asset protection, then you have the option of choosing to leave your children's inheritance in trust for the rest of their life.

At my firm, we refer to these types of Trusts as **Generational Asset Protection Trusts™ (GAPT or GAP Trusts)**. When helping our clients navigate these options, we often explain that upon the second parent's passing, your estate will be divided into separate Trusts for each of your children and that will remain in effect indefinitely after your death. Then upon your children's death, their inheritance may be passed down to your grandkids (or the remaining members of your bloodline) in "Cascading" Trusts that can live on for generations and ensure your inheritance stays in your family line. These funds can remain in GAP Trust(s) for each generation of your family, and will continue to be protected from creditors, lawsuits, and divorce.

For instance, if your child is in a car accident and is sued, the courts will not be allowed to access the assets held in a Trust. If your kids get into debt, their creditors will not be able to access the assets held in a Trust. If your child gets divorced, the assets held in the Trust will never be considered marital property and divided with their spouse. In addition, your children can grow the money left to them in an inheritance by investing, buying a home, or starting a business in the name of the Trust, which may not be counted in their estate or subject to estate tax.

When creating a GAP Trust, you can select ages where your children can manage their own Trusts by becoming a sole or co-trustee. You can choose who will serve as the trustee, co-trustee, or distribution trustee until your children are ready, or allow them to choose who should serve in these roles when you feel that they're old enough. You will also have to decide what your children can do with the Trust at the time of their death: leave everything to anyone of their choosing, allow them to leave something to their spouse or a charity, or require that everything must stay in your bloodline. The options are endless for how these Trusts can be implemented depending on your family's level of wealth and goals, but this is an advanced planning issue, and at the introductory stage of estate planning, all you need to be aware of is that a GAP Trust can provide your family with immense value and financial security to protect your children's inheritance for generations to come. Just know that each of these decisions impacts the tax effects. As a result, it would be wise to get assistance from an experienced attorney when designing the specifics and deciding whether you want your children to have control and access to their inheritance, or if you believe asset protection is more important.

A GAP Trust is the best starting point to begin creating generational wealth for your family. If it's any indication of my views on what you should do for your family, this is how my children will receive their inheritance from us. To me, it is a no-brainer because for a minimal expense, you can provide your kids with benefits that the IRS doesn't allow them to provide to themselves. They can achieve asset protection on a portion of their wealth and shield part of their estate from lawsuits, creditors, bankruptcy, and divorce, while still maintaining the right to manage and utilize their wealth—all while their inheritance may not technically be considered a part of their estate or subject to taxes, so it remains protected.

TAXES

As the old saying goes, there are only two guarantees in life: death and taxes. Estate planning lawyers put their own spin on that old adage and commonly say that the three commandments of estate planning are:

- We don't know when you'll die;
- How much money you'll have; or
- What the estate tax exemption or tax rate will be at that time.

For those of you who are new to this world and don't speak the foreign language of estate planning or love nerding out on this stuff like I do, the estate tax exemption is the amount of money you are allowed to pass down to your loved ones before the government taxes the money you leave behind. Think of it as a coupon that you can cash in at your death. The amount of the coupon changes every year, and the government sets a limit on how much money you are allowed to give away for free. Any amount that you have over the coupon amount will be taxed. There is a federal exemption, and depending on where you live, there may be an estate tax and exemption limit at the state level as well.

In Illinois, the state exemption has been $4 million since 2013.[34] The federal exemption can drastically change with each presidential administration and the passage of a new law. In

34 35 ILCS 405/2.

1916, the exemption was $50,000 and the tax rate for anything you had over that amount was taxed somewhere between 1 and 10 percent. In 2000, the exemption was $675,000, and the tax rates were between 37 and 55 percent.[35] In 2025, the exemption was changed to $15,000,000. There's no guarantee as to what these limits will be when you die, but your guess is as good as mine on whether you believe taxes will go up or down over the next few decades. Right now, the federal estate tax rate is 40 percent, but twenty-five years ago, it was 55 percent, and twenty-five years before that it was 77 percent. Regardless of what the exemption amount or tax rates may be when you pass away, no one wants to pay taxes that can easily be avoided. By establishing a Trust, your family can begin to strategically take advantage of the tax code.

For instance, if you die and leave everything to your spouse with or without a Will, then you are not using your estate tax exemption and you are effectively wasting it. Then, when your spouse dies with all your property in their name, only their exemption will apply to what they own, and we don't know what their estate tax exemption will be at that time. At this moment, you could preserve your federal exemption by "porting" it to your spouse, so they can use both your exemption and their exemption when they pass. But with a stroke of a pen, this can easily change. As I've been writing this book, the figures have increased multiple times. It all just depends on who is in power,

---

35 Tax Policy Center. "Statistics: Estate Tax Exemption Level 1916 to 2024." May 20, 2024. https://taxpolicycenter.org/statistics/estate-tax-exemption-level.

where you live, and what the amount of the estate tax exemption and tax rates happen to be in the year that each of you passes.

Right now, twelve states and the District of Columbia have an estate tax, while six states impose an inheritance tax.[36] If you live in a state that has an estate tax exemption, the rules will be different, but most states do not allow portability. So, depending on where you live and the amount of money you have, you may have to strategically plan to use each spouse's estate tax coupon at their death to avoid being taxed.

For instance, in Illinois the estate tax exemption is $4 million. If you and your spouse have $5 million in total assets (including your home, property, life insurance, retirement, banking, and financial accounts) and your spouse dies and leaves all their property to you, then when you die with $5 million, your kids will have to pay a tax bill of $285,714 to the State of Illinois.[37] However, with a little planning and a strategic Trust plan, a married couple can avoid these taxes entirely and maximize both of their exemptions, doubling the amount that they can leave behind without being taxed. In Illinois, when your spouse dies, if a portion of your assets have been placed in a "Family Trust," up to $4 million can be used to capture their "coupon" at the time of their death. Any money or assets in the Family Trust

---

36 Tax Foundation. Joseph Johns. "Estate and Inheritance Taxes by State, 2024." November 12, 2024. https://taxfoundation.org/data/all/state/estate-inheritance-taxes/.

37 Office of the Illinois Attorney General, "2013-2026 Decedents Estate Tax Calculator." https://illinoisattorneygeneral.gov/estate-taxes/2013-2025.-estate-calculator.

can grow in value over time and will not be included in the surviving spouse's estate, and the spouse will still have their own $4 million coupon to use. So, with some basic Trust planning, your family can effectively double their exemption and will not have to pay a dollar in estate taxes for assets of at least $8 million, if done correctly.

Naturally, this can get complicated quickly, but all you need to remember is that there are tax planning strategies that a professional can help you take advantage of to maximize the value of your exemption, minimize capital gains, and avoid unnecessary taxes. When it comes to asset protection, taxes, or advance planning strategies, the options are endless, and this is merely the tip of the iceberg. For now, as a starting point, I'd like for you to simply focus on getting your foundational plan in place and designing the overarching financial outcome you want for your family. Then you can consult with an experienced professional to fill in the gaps and have them educate you on the best strategies to take advantage of depending on your specific circumstances, wealth, and family dynamics to achieve your goals.

CHAPTER 9

WHAT LEGACY WILL YOU LEAVE BEHIND?

What you leave behind is not what is engraved in stone monuments, but what is woven into the lives of others.

—PERICLES

As I began writing this chapter, I received the news that a friend I'd known for decades had died. Several weeks earlier, he had collapsed and doctors had diagnosed him with cancer. In the weeks that followed, he had an operation to remove the tumor, which was deemed successful. He then began chemotherapy treatment. But it was all for nothing, and within a few short weeks of collapsing, he was gone. He was only in his late thirties.

After getting the news, the question that kept racing through my mind was *How is this possible?* An accident or self-induced problem I could comprehend, but not this. My friend had lived life to the fullest, on his own terms, with zest, eternal optimism, and a constant smile on his face. He died unable to live out his plans for the future. There was so much left unfinished, unsaid, and undone. In shock, my friends and I wondered how we could properly honor his memory, family, and legacy.

In the hours that followed, I scoured my phone and the internet for something that perfectly captured the memory of my friend. I reflected on his life, the laughs, and the memories that unfortunately weren't documented anywhere. I also thought about the regret of not seeing him for the past few years, or calling to hear about his worldwide travels, experiences, stories, and words of wisdom. It was tough coming to grips with the fact that I'd never get the chance again.

Not long after that loss, my father-in-law went to the doctor for what he thought was a pulled muscle in his abdomen and discovered a large mass was causing the pain. Within one month of his cancer diagnosis, he was gone. During those four chaotic weeks, he went through medical tests, crisis planning, and a ton of work to get his affairs in order.

My father-in-law was one of a kind and an original. He was classically private, a man of few words, and enjoyed simple pleasures. He was intelligent, set in his ways, knew what he liked, and lived life on his own terms. He was a bit of a mystery but I heard snippets of enough stories to know he lived a wild and interesting life: He moved from Illinois to Pakistan during high school, retired from the oil industry in his early 40s, traveled the world, and was infamous in Jackson Hole amongst all the ski bums. Unfortunately, all his promises to tell me the full tales over a glass of Scotch, never came to be.

In the end, those last few weeks were pretty hectic and heavy. Everything happened so fast and all our heads were spinning, so I can't imagine the stress and anxiety he was going through. When we weren't discussing medical appointments, finances, estate planning, and logistics, we simply followed his lead and did what he wanted, only hoping to make him feel comfortable and at ease. We sat around his living room, played with the kids, watched golf and the news, swapped stories, and tried to have a few laughs. When looking back on those days, the lesson that will stay with me is that I wish we'd had more time to enjoy the moment, our remaining time together, and focus on celebrating his life. I will always regret that I didn't push harder to force him to go through our planning process and document his life and legacy while he was healthy and in the right frame of mind to do so.

If you are lucky enough to have some time at the end of your life to spend with your friends and family, the last thing you'll want to do is deal with your estate planning options, beneficiary designations, burial arrangements, taxes, paperwork, finances, accounts, passwords, and usernames, while also wasting hours on hold with banks and investment advisers. In hindsight, if I had insisted on seeing my father-in-law's documents and helped him get his affairs in order earlier, it would have completely changed those final few weeks. He wouldn't have felt the additional and unnecessary stress and anxiety of addressing logistics. Instead, we would have had more time in those last few weeks together to hear his stories, words of wisdom, life lessons, and wishes.

We all have regrets about what could have been. We reflect on memories of our loved ones, the impact they've had on our lives, and the life lessons, values, and indelible marks that they've left behind. Unfortunately, those memories will eventually fade and ultimately die with us, unless we take the time to preserve them.

Ask yourself: What do you know about your great-grandparents or their parents? How much do you know about their family history, childhood, favorite memories, and the life lessons they learned by living through the Great Depression, World Wars, and adversity that would be unimaginable today? There isn't much that I know about my family history more than two to three generations back. We've been able to discover their names and where they were born and lived, but my family will never know who our ancestors truly were, what they stood for and valued, the life lessons they learned, or the wisdom they would have wanted to pass down to future generations. Their legacy has now faded into history and with time has been lost.

Please take a moment to pause and consider, if today were your last:

- What memories would you like to pass down to your children?

- What lessons or wisdom have you learned that changed your life and will also change your children's lives and future generations of your family?
- Have you preserved your family history and childhood memories of your parents and grandparents?
- Have you documented and organized your most cherished photos, videos, and memories to pass on to your kids?
- Is there anything that you have left unaddressed or unsaid?
- Is there anyone you need to thank, forgive, express your feelings, or apologize to?
- Would you take the time to create a video, letter, or message to the people you care about most to tell them how much you love them, the future that you envision for them, what you want them to remember you for, or the values, principles, and beliefs that you want them to move forward remembering and live their life by?

As we've discussed, there are so many reasons why you need to create an estate plan to protect your family. If done well and updated periodically, the traditional model of estate planning will solve a majority of the legal problems your family might face, but the intangibles are often ignored. Instead of addressing what's most important, it is a business transaction and relationship, where the answers to a few basic questions will determine what you leave behind. Simply put, it's not enough.

Your life and legacy cannot be summarized in a balance sheet or in a one-hour meeting, where the answers to a few generic questions determine what will happen to the life and legacy you've worked so hard to build. An estate plan and legal documents will often preserve your wealth, but not your wisdom. They will typically account for your money, but not your memories. Traditional documents will ensure your valuables are inherited by those you want but won't guarantee that your values are passed along with them.

THE LEGACY PLAN

Technology has left us with no excuse not to intentionally and deliberately create the legacy we wish to leave behind. Yet the digital age has also caused us to feel as if we never have enough time. We are constantly bombarded with email, voicemail, text messages, social media, and marketing messages. We are overwhelmed. Just trying to stay on top of our to-do lists seems impossible, which leaves us with little time to focus on the most important tasks in life, like preserving our most cherished memories, life lessons, and values.

That is why our process was designed to incorporate a legacy interview, where our clients begin to preserve their memories, legacy, and wisdom in their own words. During the process of creating a Family, Wealth & Legacy Plan, it is our goal to inspire our clients and give them a simple and easy system to implement so they'll periodically continue the process of documenting and storing their memories, preserving them in time for future generations. Remember, your great-grandchildren won't know how much money you left behind or the tax savings that your children enjoyed. Your legacy plan will be the only thing that will be remembered and survive more than one generation. That's why **it's crucial to intentionally design the legacy you deserve to be remembered by**.

Bear with me, but I want you to take a moment and consider a tough scenario. In those earlier examples, what if it was you who died in an accident when your children were young? You never thought you needed to preserve your memories, stories, life lessons, or family history, because you always thought you'd have more time. So the legacy, traditions, wisdom, knowledge, and values that you had hoped to pass on to your children, unfortunately, died with you.

As the years pass by, your children's memory of you starts to fade. They often look at pictures of you. On holidays and special occasions, your spouse makes it a point to show your children videos, share stories, and special memories. Yet with each passing year, these celebrations of your memory become more infrequent, and your children begin to forget the sound of your voice, your laugh, and the special moments that you cherished with them.

Years later, when your spouse starts dating and eventually remarries, your children begin to feel that the void in their lives left by your death is being filled. Or worse, your children are resentful of your spouse for remarrying and it causes a rift between them, even though you would have been happy to know that there was someone there to support and love your family.

When your children go through monumental shifts in their lives, they often wonder what it would have been like if you were there and what advice you would have given them. Unfortunately, they will never know. On their first date, prom night, graduation, engagement, wedding day, and at the birth of their first child, they are left wondering. Instead, their stepparent is in the room, and it is now their values, memories, life lessons, advice, and words of comfort that your children will receive. They will never hear your family stories, dreams for their future, memories of their birth, and all the parenting advice that you hoped to share with them when your grandchildren were born. **Let that sink in.**

Now instead, let's imagine your children were left with videos, letters, and messages telling them how much you loved them, stories about your parents, grandparents, and childhood, your greatest moments of triumph, and the lessons you learned from your greatest failures. What if you also left behind the advice that changed your life and would undoubtedly improve their lives and likelihood of success? What if you could leave behind the wisdom and guidance you would have wanted them to receive on the day they graduated from high school or college, on their wedding day, or at the birth of their first child? Imagine how it would make them feel if you weren't there to share those special moments with them. How would it impact not only their lives, but future generations of your family? How would the relationship advice you give them affect their marriage or their feelings toward your spouse when they started dating? If the unimaginable became reality for your family, what would it be worth to know that your children could fall asleep every night listening to your voice, reminded of how much you loved them, or that your great-grandchildren would be able to see you smile, hear your voice, and feel as if they knew you?

Of course, it would be better to watch the video or read the letter with your children on those special days, but if you aren't able to be there with them physically, you would still be a vital part of those important milestones. If you are fortunate enough to share in these moments, a well-thought-out letter or video that is improved over time will be much more memorable and impactful than an impromptu speech in which you uncomfortably fumble over your words and don't do justice to your true feelings of pride, love, and admiration.

As you can see, one-size-fits-all documents and the traditional transactional model of estate planning simply doesn't address what truly matters. **When it comes to your kids and the legacy you'll leave behind, there's so much more to wealth than just money.** Without a shadow of a doubt, the videos or letters you create will become your children's and grandchildren's most prized possessions and their memory of you when you are no longer here. They will allow future generations of your family to truly feel that they know you, where you came from, what you stood for, and the future that you wanted for them. Please take the time and make the effort to give your family this gift. It is invaluable and will live far beyond you if done properly. That is why we incorporate legacy planning into every Family, Wealth & Legacy Plan we prepare and encourage our clients to spend an hour or two every year building upon what they've created. In our experience, it is more impactful and beneficial than any legal strategy we could implement for our clients and matters much more to them than any of the legal documents sitting on their shelf collecting dust.

PERSONAL PROPERTY INVENTORY

If you've ever been there, then you know that after someone dies, one of the most awkward and uncomfortable steps is cleaning out their house and belongings. Family and friends are forced to spend weeks sifting through things, deciding how to divide them up, and deciphering what's treasure from trash. This experience can go one of two ways: it can either be an uncomfortable (or downright ugly) event that scars your family while they fight over your things and what you would have wanted, or it can be a great bonding experience, where your family shares fond memories of you while spending quality time together reflecting on your most prized possessions and the stories behind them.

If you walk into my parent's home right now, you'd see how every wall is filled floor to ceiling with pictures, and every shelf is filled with tchotchkes. My parents have traveled the world, and my dad loves buying souvenirs. Every piece of art and trinket has a story behind it that my parents treasure. Yet, if my brother and I were forced to clean out my parents' home, we wouldn't know where 95 percent of these things came from or the memories behind them. We'd question what to do with this massive amount of "stuff." We wouldn't know if their best friends, or a relative, had gone a trip with them and would love to receive that small memento to remember my parents by. We wouldn't remember the stories behind the childhood toys that they've held onto for over forty years. We would have a difficult time going through it all, and it would be an overwhelming and frustrating burden. Even worse, in the end, most of our parents' cherished items would sadly be donated to Goodwill or thrown in the trash.

Now imagine that my parents went through their home and made a list of all the important things that they owned, the story behind each item, and who they wanted to inherit it. It would change everything. My brother and I would know what's important and what isn't. We would go from room to room sharing all the stories behind our parents' belongings with their grandchildren. We would laugh and shed a few tears together, reflecting on a home full of memories and all the stories these "things" told. We would make sure that the people who would cherish these items the most got them, as my parents would have wanted. Instead of getting upset or feeling like we were burdened with the task of dealing with their stuff, we would create an unforgettable memory, bonding over our love for our parents and celebrating their lives.

When creating a Family, Wealth & Legacy Plan, we give our clients a legally valid document that allows them to easily identify all the valuable items they own and who should receive them. We also provide them with a system and instructions to regularly update this list throughout their lives. In real-time, they can add to their personal property inventory and capture memories that they hold dear in their hearts—in writing, with photos or videos—so that these important items and the stories behind them will remain in their family for generations to come. Imagine you have a video of you and your three-year-old playing with their favorite toy and attach a link to it on your inventory. How will it feel to know that thirty years later, whether you are alive or not, your grandkids will be able to watch that unforgettable memory you shared with your kids when it is passed down to them? These things matter and will shape the life and legacy you leave behind.

This really hit home for me recently when my mother gave me a toy that she clearly cherished. It had my name on it and played a song. As she reminisced, I could tell that it clearly meant a lot to her, but I have no memory of it. Every kid has those few special toys, and every parent vividly remembers their tiny toddler's adorable obsession with them, along with that song that was stuck in your head for years after hearing it for the millionth time. The question you should ask yourself is: Will they remember when going through your old boxes? Or will it simply be dismissed as junk and thrown away?

END-OF-LIFE DECISIONS

Planning a funeral is always difficult for families. There are so many arrangements to be made and costs that are incurred. Families are burdened with decisions surrounding cremation, burial, cemetery location, selection of a funeral home, a coffin, pallbearers, who to ask to give the eulogy, songs to be played, photos to display, flower arrangements, writing an obituary, and much more. During the process of planning, we help our clients start thinking about these issues and documenting their wishes. We also guide them on various financial strategies that can be built into their plan to ensure that their family can access the funds they need to pay for these costs. In the end, we give our clients the tools and assistance, so that when the time comes, this process is as easy as possible for their families.

If you don't have a plan, your family will be left to make these decisions without your input. They will need to pay all these costs themselves, and then they will also incur attorney's fees to request that the court approve a reimbursement from your estate. It will make a challenging and stressful time that much more difficult for your family, not only emotionally but also financially. Please take the time and make the effort to ease this burden on them and to ensure that the last representation of your life is something you would have wanted.

DESIGN YOUR LEGACY

Let's face facts: We're all going to die one day. Our time on earth is brief, but that's what makes it beautiful and precious. In the end, your memory and your legacy are all that you will leave behind. The question is what are you going to do to design the legacy you will leave behind? **It is within your power and control to intentionally design how you want to be remembered.**

By making an investment of your time and effort, you can give your family this invaluable gift. We've covered a lot, but start where you are, pick a small attainable task to tackle, set a date or a deadline to get it done, and build traditions where you and your family can commit to complete whatever you feel may be most impactful for generations to come. Over the decades, you'll be amazed at what you can accomplish by investing a few hours each year. Don't wait, because the biggest mistake we can make in life is thinking we have more time.

SECTION 4

ARE YOU READY FOR DIVORCE?

Divorce sucks. There is no sugarcoating it. It's terrible. But it doesn't have to be the next World War, either. What if you could get help to approach it strategically, feel supported, and have cordial conversations? You can navigate divorce in a way that doesn't destroy your family financially and emotionally. There are several alternative, private, collaborative, and respectful alternatives, where couples can divorce with dignity and preserve the integrity of their relationship in a process that is generally much faster, less expensive, and done completely outside of court.

CHAPTER 10

PREPARING FOR A SUCCESSFUL DIVORCE

Our greatest joy and our greatest pain comes in our relationships with others.

—STEPHEN R. COVEY

People don't get married expecting to be unhappy or that they'll ever get divorced. As newlyweds, everyone expects to grow old together and live happily ever after. But for decades, the divorce rate in the United States has hovered around 50 percent, and half of all children will witness their parents' divorce. So it's wise to know what your friends, family, or even your kids may be in for if they find themselves on the wrong side of the statistics.[38,39,40]

Far too often, people rush into the decision to initiate a divorce based on emotion and external factors, but how you handle those first steps will determine the direction of your life and the lives of your children. ***Research shows that the death of a parent has a less harmful effect on kids than their parents' divorce***, but those harmful effects can be minimized based on how a couple conducts themselves during the process. So, for your children's sake, please take the time to do your research, evaluate your options, prepare, and do the hard work needed to ensure you get the outcome your family deserves.

GETTING PERSONAL

My mother-in-law married her accountant in her late fifties. She was an elementary school teacher and was led to believe the man she was marrying was a successful and wealthy owner of his own accounting firm. Not long after I asked my wife to marry me,

---

38 Morrow-Kondos, D. "How Kids See Death and Divorce." Tulsa Kids. (July 27, 2016). https://www.tulsakids.com/how-kids-see-death-and-divorce/#:~:text=This%20study%20has%20found%20that,many%20years%20into%20the%20future.%E2%80%9D.

39 American Academy of Child and Adolescent Psychiatry. "Children and Divorce." (2017, January). www.aacap.org/AACAP/Families_and_Youth/Facts_for_Families/FFF-Guide/Children-and-Divorce-001.aspx.

40 U.S. Centers for Disease Control and Prevention (CDC). National Vital Statistics Systems. "Marriages and Divorces." (March 7, 2024). https://www.cdc.gov/nchs/nvss/marriage-divorce.htm.

her stepdad filed for divorce from my mother-in-law. Go figure. He filed before the divorce attorney officially became a member of the family.

When he filed for divorce after ten years of marriage, it took over a month to track down my mother-in-law's money, because her husband had moved her accounts so many times. Once we found them, she was devastated to learn that 70 percent of her life savings had been spent or lost in poor investments by her soon-to-be ex-husband. So, instead of tripling her money along with the market, she was only left with 30 percent of what she had brought into the marriage. On top of that, he was now demanding half of what was left of her assets because, in his words, "it was marital property, it is the law, and he was broke."

My wife and I spent the next five years (yes, it took that long to litigate) trying to obtain and poring over more than 30,000 pages of financial documents. After we put all the pieces together, we came to the conclusion that he knew the law, deliberately planned what he had done, conned my mother-in-law, and used his attorney and financial adviser friends to trick her into turning over control of her money.[41] Once the liquid money was gone (and a divorce attorney was about to come into the family), he filed for divorce rather than admit there wasn't any money left to contribute to the wedding.

---

41 Legal disclaimer: This is only my opinion and in no way a certain fact. Yet, after five years of eating, breathing, and sleeping this case, I stand by my opinion, which was set forth in great detail at trial.

After those five years of litigation, he spent more than $300,000 in attorney's fees and lost every meaningful issue brought before the court. My mother-in-law spent more than $50,000 on a financial expert, which would have cost an additional $150,000+ if my wife hadn't done all the accounting behind the scenes. Had my mother-in-law retained another divorce attorney, her case would never have gotten the attention and level of detail that we put into it. If that same attorney had devoted the exact amount time that we spent working on her case, her legal bill would have easily exceeded $500,000. She only paid a fraction of that to cover the attorney's fees for my co-counsel and my staff's costs.

It was a rough few years for my family. My wife and I did our absolute best to shield her mother from having to deal with the case because she was already so distraught and we didn't want it to affect her any more than it already had. Thankfully, we received the best result we possibly could have and closed that chapter of our lives.

In hindsight, that experience gave meaning to the wise words that our worst days and biggest problems in life can be our greatest gift. If my grandmother or my mother-in-law had found someone like me when they'd needed it, and had established an estate plan and invested the time and money to find an attorney and trusted resource to advise them, my mother-in-law never would have let her ex-husband near her money, and we wouldn't have had to go through that ordeal. If our family hadn't gone through those difficult years, I wouldn't have been inspired to change my life, my practice, and my mission to help others avoid experiencing the same fate. It was my mother-in-law's case that forced me to seek out a better way and a new alternative for my clients. It was the catalyst and what motivated me to get certified in mediation and collaborative law, and at the conclusion of her case, I never accepted another contested divorce case that was going to be litigated in the traditional courtroom setting.

WHERE TO START

Not too infrequently, a friend, colleague, or former client will call in a panic, worried about the possibility of getting divorced. The first thing I do is ask what happened. After they're done explaining everything that's ever gone wrong in their marriage (to the only person they know who legitimately can't tell anyone else because it's confidential), I inquire if they think there's any way to save their marriage. We discuss their goals and what they really want their future to look like five to ten years from now. Then I ask them if they think it would be wise to take some time before making a decision, because divorce is not something to be taken lightly.

My next piece of advice is always to start the process of contemplating divorce by seeing a counselor individually, as a couple, or both. Here are a few of the reasons why therapy can be invaluable when considering divorce.

Self-Reflection

Unhappy people often blame everyone and everything around them for their own baggage. No one other than you can make you happy, and divorce may not be the answer or solution to your problems. A good counselor can help you take a long look in the mirror and encourage you to carefully consider your options and the ramifications of this life-changing decision.

Self-improvement

No matter what you're going through, individual counseling will offer you a support system and provide you with professional guidance and advice regarding your relationship, along with some tools to improve your communication skills and stress (or anger) management. Having a trusted resource for advice and someone to lean on as a sounding board while you navigate working on your marriage or face the prospect of divorce, will be invaluable.

Saving the Marriage

You should make a good faith effort to save your marriage with the support of a professional and go to couple's counseling. It will offer a healthy and safe environment where you can discuss your relationship and how you and your spouse want to move forward. Naturally, this only applies if the police aren't involved, everyone's safe, and no one walked in on some crazy *Eyes Wide Shut* moment. But, if it's possible, give your spouse, your marriage, and potentially your children the respect your family deserves because one person is often much further along in the process. Taking some time to make a good faith effort to save your marriage and then easing into the idea of separation can soften the blow and go a long way in allowing a couple to begin discussing divorce peacefully.

Discussing Divorce

This will offer the best possible environment to have a difficult, but mature conversation, while you both take the necessary time and space to come to terms with the idea of divorce in between meetings. Counseling can provide a forum for spouses to begin discussing their wish to separate, the reasons, their goals, and their expectations of what life might look like during separation or after divorce. If you choose the right therapist, they will be knowledgeable enough to help you begin negotiating terms of the divorce, temporary agreements, and parenting schedules to experiment with, and give suggestions on what should or shouldn't be said to the children. It can also allow a couple to respectfully discuss their options on how to proceed in a civil manner.

Cost

Insurance will likely cover the cost of counseling and all you'll be responsible for is a mere copay, while an attorney or divorce coach will charge you a significantly higher hourly rate. When preparing for and going through the divorce process, having professionals to lean on will be invaluable as you navigate a traumatic and difficult time. There will be a lot to work through that has nothing to do with the law. A good therapist can help you mentally prepare for the journey, work through unresolved emotions, improve communication, and can be a trusted resource to talk through non-legal issues. You never want to use your attorney as your therapist, trust me. We aren't educated or trained to do so, and our hourly rate is astronomically higher. You also don't want to burden your friends and family with the role of your therapist and legal adviser; they aren't qualified and it may strain your relationships with loved ones. So, if you have any reservations about therapy, suck it up and do it anyway. In the end, it will save you a lot of money, time, and potentially years in divorce court.

HOW TO PREPARE FOR DIVORCE

Once someone has made the decision to proceed with a divorce, my advice is that they need to get prepared. Before embarking on this journey, they need to know where they are and where they want to go so they can evaluate their options, map out their route, and end up at the destination they intended. To properly prepare, please follow our S.M.A.R.T. Divorce Framework™.

Set Your Goals

One of the most important steps in preparing for divorce is to sit down and write out what you want your life to look like, so please go back to Chapter 1 and complete the exercise, but be specific to your life post-divorce. Ask yourself:

- How do you want to conduct yourself during the process?
- How do you want to look back on this experience years from now, and what memories will stick with you?
- How will your children remember this difficult period in their lives?
- What example are you going to set for your children, and how will it impact their future relationships?
- What do you want your relationship with your ex to look like?
- What do you want your relationships with family, friends, and in-laws to be like after the divorce is over?
- What do you want your children's graduations, weddings, holidays, and the birth of your first grandchild to look like? To feel like?
- Will both you and your spouse be invited to your grandchildren's celebrations and holidays, or will your children be burdened with choosing between you?

You are about to embark on a life-changing transition that will define the quality of your life moving forward. Don't let fear, worry, or anger cloud your judgment or cause you to do something that you may regret in the heat of an emotional moment. Take the time to step back, focus on the big picture, and think about what you truly want. Just remember to stay optimistic and imagine the best-case scenario. Once you've created a vision of what you want for your family's future, you can start focusing on how to approach your divorce in the present. It will change the way you approach conversations with your spouse, how you treat them, the tone of voice you use, and the level of compromise, patience, and care you show them. If you have kids, then please remember to put them first. Your future relationship with them and their well-being depends on your ability to coparent and coexist with your soon-to-be ex in a healthy manner for decades to come. More importantly, please remember what you read above: "Research shows that the death of a parent has a less harmful effect on children than their parents' divorce." You may not be able to shield your children from every consequence, but you can put their well-being above all else, focus consciously on how best to support them through the process, protect them from unnecessary conflict, and significantly reduce the lasting harm caused by your divorce.

If it's feasible, you may even want to carefully select and share a portion of your goals with your spouse. It may go a long way to show them that you want the best for them and your children as you begin this difficult journey. By sharing mutually beneficial and considerate goals, you can diffuse their worries and speculation about your motives and potentially even agree on mutual goals and the process that you'd like to utilize prior to taking any action. This will allow you to start the process with agreement, and move forward with an aligned vision for your future, your divorce, and how you wish to approach it for the sake of your kids. When negotiations get difficult or things get heated down the road, coming back to these shared goals can bring the temperature down and remind you both of what's most important, allowing for compromise in the midst of conflict.

Mentally Prepare

My experience has shown me that the drama, expense, and delay associated with a divorce typically follows the 80/20 rule. Only 20 percent of the issues are related to the legal side of things, while the other 80 percent stem from unresolved emotional and deeply personal issues. When a couple has done the hard work on their relationship and begun to civilly discuss the legal issues that will arise, they can resolve their divorce with significantly less negative impact to themselves and their children.

Your attitude, behavior, and the choices you make during divorce will affect your life for decades. How you conduct yourself during these critical times will determine your future well-being financially, emotionally, and in your relationships. That is why it is so important to mentally prepare yourself for the fact that you are going to be forced to make very important decisions that will affect your future, at a time of great stress, when you may not feel equipped to do so. Your ability to negotiate calmly, reason logically, and achieve a mutually beneficial and successful outcome for your family will depend on your preparation and self-control.

Assemble Your Documents

Collect or electronically save copies of your financial and personal records. At a minimum, this should include three years of tax returns, W-2s, 1099s and the prior year-end paycheck stubs for you and your spouse, along with the current statements for all your financial accounts, investments, and debts. If you can find them, also gather any records of the assets that you had in the month before you got married. If the account passwords are changed or the papers disappear from the filing cabinet during your divorce, it will be helpful and having these documents will reduce the difficulty, anxiety, and attorney's fees involved with getting them from your spouse later.

Gather your documents and save them while it's still convenient and easy to do. If you have any suspicion that there may have been any funny business going on with your money, then collect the past few years' worth of banking, investment, and retirement statements. Ideally, you'll save your documents electronically so they can easily be accessed and provided to the professionals when needed. You don't want to pay for legal staff to spend hours scanning and organizing all the statements for you. If that's not in the cards and you can't save digital copies, then minimally, make a paper copy and put the statements back where you found them so your spouse doesn't lose access or get suspicious.

Review Your Numbers

Create a balance sheet with all of your assets and debts. This will help you get financially organized and provides you with a simple overview of everything you own and owe on one page. It will help facilitate realistic discussions based on actual numbers. It will also save you a great deal of time and attorney's fees if this is created before meeting with a lawyer. This simple document allows a couple, or their attorneys, to generate options and realistic solutions to settle a case quickly, efficiently, and at the lowest cost.

Download your free copy of the Marital Balance Sheet that we use in our cases at www.fwlls.com/life-happens-are-you-ready.

Take Financial Action

When preparing for divorce, you should also set aside enough money to pay for it. People plan and budget for their wedding, but they never seem to do the same for a divorce. Divorce isn't cheap, regardless of what option you choose. Like buying a house or a car, there are cheap and expensive models, different features, and pros and cons to each choice, so you'll need to know what your options are and what you can afford. If you know your numbers, you can show them to your attorney and honestly discuss costs, and if possible, you should also do so with your spouse. Attorneys don't work for free and you and your spouse are paying for both of your attorneys out of one pot of money. Be mindful that every telephone call, meeting, email, and court appearance costs money that could be divided between you and your spouse. The last thing you want to do is put yourself in debt that you can't manage during a divorce, because it will only lead to more anxiety and negative emotions during an already difficult time. For example, regardless of the approach you take to your divorce, at a minimum, you will most likely pay filing fees to the court that are in the range of $500 to $1,000, and those are merely the county fees to file the petition and an appearance on behalf of both parties.

Not only will the divorce be expensive, but the amount of income you've grown accustomed to having, and which only supported one household, is going to have to support two following the divorce. To make this work, your monthly expenses are going to need to be cut. While you are in the initial stages of preparing for divorce, it's crucial that you understand your monthly budget and what you're spending on necessities and luxuries to maintain the lifestyle you and your spouse are accustomed to. That is the only way you will be able to realistically negotiate based on the facts and actual numbers, rather than emotions. Debt makes it that much worse, so if you have any marital credit card debt and the ability to pay it off, you should. Please discuss this with your spouse first to avoid unnecessary arguments or suspicion, but this will reduce your expenses and increase your credit scores. In addition, if you need to apply for a new credit card, refinance your home, purchase or rent a home or a new vehicle, apply as "married" with your total household income while you still can, and prior to a petition being filed in court. If you do, you'll qualify for much more than you will as an individual post-divorce. Don't put these decisions off. If you put in the time, effort, and hard work to properly prepare, it will reduce the amount of work for your attorneys during the divorce and lower the cost for your family.

THE FIVE RULES OF DIVORCE COMMUNICATION

Healthy communication is the primary and driving factor to an "easy," quicker, and less expensive divorce. Unfortunately, it is also typically the source of marital problems, so whatever you've been doing will probably need to change. It may be a Herculean effort to improve your communication and break old habits, but it will be well worth it. My advice is to work with a professional on communicating with your spouse in a healthy and productive manner. To help get you started, here is the advice I always give to clients.

1. Be Realistic

People's perception of the law is based on television and movies, but that isn't how it works in real life. **Attorneys, judges, and the legal process are not going to provide you with the vengeance, vindication, justice, or retribution that you may be seeking.** It doesn't matter who filed for divorce, was unfaithful, or made the decision to split up, and none of that is factored into the result. Tough talk and threatening your spouse at the beginning of a divorce isn't going to get you anywhere. It will only make matters worse. **You need to treat divorce like a business transaction because that is what it is.** In the eyes of the law, you are dissolving a contractual relationship. The judge doesn't care why you're angry or upset; everyone in their courtroom is angry for one reason or another.

To negotiate effectively during a divorce, you'll need to understand what result is most likely to unfold before you begin throwing around demands. This will allow your communications with your spouse to be more productive and come from an educated point of view.

It is also human nature that once you take a strong position, make a demand, or draw a line in the sand, it becomes much harder to walk it back later. Psychologically, accepting anything less may begin to feel like a loss, even if you didn't know any better at the time. If you later discover that your demand was unrealistic or inconsistent with how things typically play out in the legal system, being forced to reverse course may undermine your credibility, rapport, and standing with your spouse.

In my experience, people spend months, if not years, fighting over issues that could easily be avoided if they simply weighed the cost-benefit analysis and knew their numbers. People often told me that it is the "principle" that matters and that they'd rather pay me than their spouse, but in the end, they spend ten times the value of an asset, debt, or issue arguing about it instead of coming to a reasonable agreement. What you need to keep in mind is that **the "principle" won't end your case, improve your relationship, increase your bank account, or allow you to move on with your life.** If you can be realistic and reasonable throughout the process and objectively evaluate the cost of conflict over compromise, you can avoid spending months, years, and your life savings fighting over issues that can be avoided.

2. Ask Questions, Don't Make Statements

This is typically my first piece of advice for men, because listening without offering an opinion isn't typically our strong suit. By simply asking questions and following up to inquire why the other person feels the way they do, you can learn a lot about what they're really thinking but aren't willing to come out and tell you initially. You'll begin to understand their point of view, what they really want, and why they want it. This will allow you to gather a lot of helpful information, generate options, reality test, and find reasonable solutions down the road that you may have never thought of.

There is a big difference in saying, "Here's my proposal; it's fair and you need to agree," versus asking, "What do you think would be fair?" and following up with, "Why do you feel that way?" or, "Have you considered…?" or, "Do you think it'd be fair if…?" Let what you hear in response marinate. Don't react, place judgment, or offer your opinion. Just listen and wait to generate solutions on your own later. Then, after reflecting on what they told you in prior conversations and brainstorming potential solutions that would appeal to both of you, go back and ask more questions.

3. Be an Active Listener

Active listening is a valuable tool in communication. If you pay attention to what people say and repeat it back to them without judgment, it will make them feel that you have heard and understood them. It creates rapport and allows you to negotiate more effectively. For example, before you respond to anyone, take a moment and reflect on what they said by saying, "If I'm hearing you correctly, you feel that…is that accurate?"

4. Compliment and Find Value

Everyone has the desire to feel understood, heard, and valued. A simple "thank you," compliment, or expression of your appreciation can go a long way. If you can find merit in another person's opinion, even if you don't agree, it will foster respectful communication, allowing a greater opportunity for compromise and agreement.

5. Document Your Agreements

While you are in the initial stages of divorce, if you and your spouse can come to agreement on any particular issue, write it down (exchange an email, a working document, or a signed piece of paper), and track your ongoing agreements. By doing so, you're tracking your progress and creating a paper trail of your discussions, agreements, and any action items that need to be accomplished. Because it's written down, it will hold everyone accountable and avoid potential misunderstandings and disagreements down the road. Just remember, with every agreement, you are making progress and saving time and attorney's fees, so acknowledge and celebrate any progress that is made. **These "kitchen table" negotiations are the cheapest and most efficient way to resolve your divorce.** However, if one side is acting inappropriately or pressuring the other, it can destroy any remaining trust, good faith, and willingness to have future discussions...so you have to be careful and tread lightly when managing settlement negotiations.

WHAT MAKES MEETINGS SUCCESSFUL

Based on my experience, the most successful settlement discussions should occur in person (or minimally, via Zoom). Email, text, and written communication can often cause misunderstandings or come across differently than intended. My advice is do whatever you need to do to appeal to your spouse and politely ask them if you can schedule a meeting to discuss a fair and amicable solution. If they agree to meet, make sure you follow the seven rules for a successful meeting:

1. **Set Ground Rules:** Before every meeting, you should start by agreeing to ground rules, including refraining from using inappropriate language, insults, and accusations, or focusing on the past. If possible, you should write these rules down, and then use that agreed upon list to bring down the temperature when things get heated. Naturally, you know your audience here. I don't want you to make this too formal or weird because it's

not a business meeting, but you know each other's hot buttons, so regardless of whether they are written down, agreed to in advance, or informally discussed as you start to chat, please address the obvious things up front and set a baseline to keep the meeting civil and productive.

2. **Create an Agenda:** Prepare a list of issues to be discussed in advance of each meeting and stick to the list. If you exchange your list in advance, you can collaborate on what issues are the highest priority and need to be addressed, or you can start by asking each other's opinion and making the list right then and there. Whatever you do, avoid meandering from topic to topic and reliving the typical highlight reel of disagreements and past grievances. You have a small window to show your spouse that you're willing to treat them fairly, communicate in a healthy manner, and cooperate. If you don't quickly make progress and start to build a bridge, it's unlikely that either one of you will be willing to sit down for a second meeting.

3. **Limit the Meeting Length:** Meetings should not last more than one to two hours. In addition, you both need to prioritize these meetings and commit to the time scheduled. Don't schedule anything that could interfere with the time allotted, require you to cut the meeting short, or make you cancel at the last minute.

4. **Neutral Meeting Locations:** Meetings should be conducted in a safe environment. Depending on your ability to keep things civil, these meetings can be

conducted in the privacy of your home, but if you want everyone to be on their best behavior, my suggestion is to conduct your meetings during a counseling session or in public (at a restaurant or over coffee).

5. **Addressing Disagreements:** At the beginning of each meeting, you should mutually agree that if a dispute arises on any particular issue, you will note it and simply move on to the next. For any issues that remain unresolved, decide together how you will handle them. My suggestion is that you each generate three acceptable options and the reasons you think each option is fair so you can discuss them at a follow-up meeting. If you're at an impasse, take your list to a professional and get some help on the last few issues. Whatever you do, just please remember to stay calm and focus on the outcome you want in the long run. A single outburst or heated moment can destroy your ability to negotiate effectively and continue an unhealthy dialogue with your spouse for decades to come.
6. **Schedule the Next Meeting:** Always schedule the next meeting before you leave. I highly recommend scheduling at least two meetings, so there is always a backup on the books, just in case someone needs to cancel.
7. **Celebrate Your Wins:** You should acknowledge and celebrate your progress at the end of each meeting because, in just a few hours, you probably saved enough money to pay for a tropical vacation after your divorce, instead of buying one for your attorney. A simple "thank

you" and a genuine expression of your appreciation and gratitude can go a long way in building rapport and set the tone for future meetings.

CHAPTER 11

LEGAL ISSUES ADDRESSED IN DIVORCE

Success depends upon previous preparation, and without such preparation there is sure to be failure.

—CONFUCIUS

The world of divorce is foreign to most people. This complex area of the law has its own language, customs, and norms. You'll need to consult with an attorney or mediator in your local area to fully understand the intricacies and to act as your translator. But before you do, I'd like to share a few key concepts and issues that will be addressed during your negotiations.

PARENTING TIME AND DECISION-MAKING

If you have kids under the age of eighteen, you're going to have to deal with the issues of parenting time, decision-making, parental responsibilities, and custody. Regardless of what this may be called in your state, it ultimately means deciding who the kids are going to live with, what their schedule with each parent is going to be from day-to-day, where they go on holidays, and who gets to make decisions regarding their well-being, education, health care, religion, and activities. Children should never become pawns in a divorce or affect financial negotiations, and that is why parenting issues should always be resolved first.

Every state and courthouse across America have a different, run-of-the-mill way that they use to settle most of the parenting cases that come before them. Over the course of my career, these standards and norms have changed every few years. Twenty years ago, the continuing legal education we received from child psychologists would be deemed extremely harmful to children today. For example, they used to tell us that kids needed to be in the same home and go through the same routine on school nights. This led to a standard where dads got alternating weekends and one or two dinners per week with their kids. Twenty years later, we're seeing a trend of encouraging 50/50 parenting schedules, where the kids become nomads traveling between homes throughout the week, because experts say that children are resilient.[42]

Regardless of the reason for shifting trends in the psychological research over the years, when it comes to raising kids, I don't know what to believe anymore. Quite frankly, the only thing that I can say with certainty is that when it comes to your family, there is no one-size-fits-all approach to parenting or your kids. My daughter's needs, routine, and optimal schedule is going to be very different from what is best for your kids. That's why these extremely important decisions should be made by your family, instead of by a judge who doesn't know you or your children.

My recommendation is that you avoid allowing a judge to implement a standard schedule that is applied to the hundreds, if not thousands, of families passing through their courtroom every year. Instead, you should address parenting issues with a therapist in your area who is extremely familiar with divorce, preferably someone who is certified in collaborative law as a Child or Family Specialist. This specialist will help you navigate these discussions in a healthy environment where you can raise your concerns, experiment with various schedules, and agree on the best approach for your family and your children. It will cost much less than using an attorney at a higher hourly rate, and they will be knowledgeable in child development,

---

42 Daniel Fernandez-Kranz. "The impact of equal parenting time laws on family outcomes and risky behavior by teenagers: Evidence from Spain." *Journal of Economic Behavior & Organization*, Volume 195, March 2022, p. 303-325. https://www.sciencedirect.com/science/article/abs/pii/S0167268122000075.

psychology, the court process, decisions that need to be made, and the standards in your local courthouse. By using a trained collaborative child specialist, you are getting the best of both worlds (legal and mental health). And honestly, they're typically much nicer and more patient than attorneys.

In Illinois, there is one organization that is responsible for training and overseeing every collaborative professional in the state: Collaborative Divorce Illinois.[43] On their website, you can find every member and trained child specialist or coach in Illinois. Most states have a similar organization, and the professionals in your local area can easily be found through a simple Google search. There's nothing stopping you and your spouse from jointly interviewing and hiring a child specialist before you ever retain an attorney. If you do, they can help you to begin resolving one of the most challenging issues before your divorce ever begins. Then, when you're ready, someone you now know and trust can recommend collaborative and settlement-focused attorneys in your area.

If you can't find collaboratively trained attorneys or a child specialist in your area, then I'd recommend focusing on finding a mediator. Preferably this is someone who is an attorney, but the focus of their practice is helping families resolve their cases by agreement and outside of court. If their website and marketing clearly focus on this approach, then you're on the right track. If their messaging is all about aggressive representation,

---

43 Collaborative Divorce Illinois (2025). https://collaborativedivorceillinois.org/.

protection, and winning, you may want to keep looking. Then, when you're interviewing potential attorneys who are also trained in mediation, ask if they know any good therapists in the area who can assist them in the process. If they work closely with the therapist on a regular basis, even better. In essence, when the attorney and the therapist are communicating and working together, you've created your own pseudo-collaborative and uncontested process. This will allow you to create a support system for your family and a team of people to lean on if any parenting-related arguments arise in years to come.

Just remember that parenting issues are naturally the most personal and difficult to resolve in a divorce. During marriage, a couple fulfills different roles and responsibilities. Post-divorce, those roles will change, your schedules will change, and as hard as it may be, both parents are going to need to cooperate for the sake of the kids. You may have concerns, apprehensions, and fears about relinquishing certain parenting responsibilities to your ex-spouse, but your life is going to change, and you are going to need help and a break once in a while (to run errands, deal with emergencies, or even go on date *with someone else*).

Studies show that having both parents actively involved in a child's life can provide significant academic, emotional, social, psychological, and health benefits, which offer a greater likelihood of success later in life.[44, 45, 46] So, please be open-minded, use a child specialist to voice your concerns, and experiment with different parenting schedules and responsibilities while building trust as co-parents over time. It won't be easy. However, if you build a team and a support system of experienced professionals, who genuinely care about both of your best interests, they can help you navigate through some difficult moments. They can serve as "the bad guys" on your behalf, explore options, reality test, or build the bridge between you when trying to negotiate a mutually beneficial agreement.

We're all hyperprotective of our kids and their well-being, but when it comes to your soon-to-be ex-spouse, you're going to have to give them a chance to prove themselves and step up to be a full-time parent. The alternative is to spend years of your life and your children's college tuition fighting over these issues

---

44 D'Onofrio, B., & Emery, R. (2019). "Parental divorce or separation and children's mental health." *World Psychiatry: Official Journal of the World Psychiatric Association (WPA), 18*(1), 100–101. National Institutes of Health, National Library of Medicine: National Center for Biotechnology Information. https://doi.org/10.1002/wps.20590.

45 Clark, B., & Canadian Paediatric Society, Mental Health and Developmental Disabilities Committee (2013). "Supporting the mental health of children and youth of separating parents." Paediatrics & child health, 18(7), 373–377. National Institutes of Health, National Library of Medicine: National Center for Biotechnology Information.

46 Meinou H.C. Theunissen, Mariska Klein Velderman, Anne P.G. Cloostermans, Sijmen A. Reijneveld. "Emotional and behavioural problems in young children with divorced parents." *European Journal of Public Health*, Volume 27, Issue 5, October 2017, Pages 840–845. https://doi.org/10.1093/eurpub/ckx056.

in court, while also destroying your ability to co-parent and maintain a decent working relationship.

CHILD SUPPORT

The calculation of child support is dependent on your state laws, but typically the parenting schedule and each spouse's income will affect the amount of child support to be paid. It is helpful to do a little bit of research on your state law before you begin negotiating a parenting schedule so you know how it may impact child support before you set a precedent that can't be undone.

Depending on what state you live in, you may be able to find an online child support calculator to give you an estimate. A simple search for "Illinois child support calculator" leads you right to a government website that can offer you a rough estimate of what to expect.[47] That being said, my thought has always been that support is an issue that should be addressed with an attorney (or mediator) and is usually not negotiable, but rather a mathematical calculation that is out of your control. There's a lot of specific information and data points that can drastically affect support that an experienced professional will be aware of. Support calculations can be manipulated and there's a lot that goes into it—that's why I'll never use the online calculators because the numbers are never the same as a more detailed calculation that

---

47 Illinois Department of Healthcare and Family Services: Child Support Services. "Illinois Child Support Estimator," (2025). https://cscwebext.hfs.illinois.gov/CscWebEx/app/estimator?execution=e1s1.

my office would run through our software. Additionally, you need to know that over and above child support, typically both parents will also be required to contribute to certain expenses for the kids, including health insurance and their medical, educational, extra-curricular, childcare, and college expenses.

SPOUSAL SUPPORT (AKA MAINTENANCE OR ALIMONY)

When it comes to spousal support, your state law will determine how it's calculated, the amount to be paid, and the duration. For your purposes, it's safe to assume that the longer you were married, the longer the time frame, and the greater the disparity in your earnings, the greater the amount that will need to be paid. If you are curious about the amount or duration of spousal support, a Google search will likely lead you to your state's rules, and possibly even a calculator where you can get a rough estimate.[48] To get an accurate number, you should address this issue with an attorney (or mediator), but without a prenup, the amount is also typically outside of your control.

While we're on the subject, one of the primary reasons to consider a prenup (or a premarital agreement) is to opt out of your state's standards for what is known as maintenance, alimony, or spousal support. As you learned in Chapter 2, prenuptial agreements can accomplish a lot of things:

---

48 Illinois Department of Healthcare and Family Services: Child Support Services. "Illinois Child Support Estimator," (2025).https://cscwebext.hfs.illinois.gov/CscWebEx/app/csc?execution=e4s1.

- How you will manage your finances post-marriage
- The definition of marital and non-marital property
- Protecting non-marital assets
- Safeguarding family businesses
- Exempting any future inheritance

But defining *how* spousal support will be calculated is one of the primary reasons that many of my clients elect to negotiate a premarital agreement prior to walking down the aisle. Otherwise, you are subjecting yourself to your state's default rules on how your family's finances may be divided in the event of divorce.

PROPERTY DIVISION

As a general rule, each spouse will receive 50 percent of the value of the marital estate, so if you create a balance sheet and compile all the current balances, you should be able to start identifying how you can divide everything fairly. There's a lot that goes into this, and it is helpful to consult with an attorney, mediator, or financial specialist (also called a financial neutral), but the more work you can do to prepare, the less the divorce will cost in the end. So, here are a few of the key concepts you should understand:

1. Marital Versus Non-marital

Understanding your state's definition of marital and non-marital property is essential to begin determining what makes up your marital estate. This will be dependent on your state's laws and whether you are in a "community property" or "separate property" state. Illinois is a separate property state, but similarly, marital property is defined as anything acquired by either spouse following the date of marriage, including assets, debts, income, businesses, and retirement accounts.[49] It doesn't matter whose name is on the account or who holds the title. If it was acquired during marriage, it's presumed to be marital property.[50]

In Illinois, non-marital property includes anything you had before the marriage, gifts, or inheritance received during the marriage that is in your name only, and the increase in value of any non-marital property.[51] The law in Illinois is that your property is presumed to be marital, so you will need proof that it's non-marital and that marital money wasn't mixed (or "commingled") with your non-marital funds.[52] This can be one of the most common and difficult issues to address in a divorce, because, frankly, it goes against common sense. Married couples often want to put things in a joint account or put their beloved on the title to their house, but in doing so they convert (or "transmute") what was non-marital into marital property. They then get very upset when their attorney explains how they voluntarily converted their non-marital property to marital property and now have to divide it with their spouse, simply because they didn't know any better. For instance, if you own a

---

49 750 ILCS 5/503(a).

50 750 ILCS 5/503(b)(1).

51 750 ILCS 5/503(a).

52 750 ILCS 5/503(c).

home before you get married and then, decades down the road, you refinance and put your spouse's name on the title, you have magically "gifted" your non-marital home to the marriage under the law. If you deposit your inheritance into a joint account and mix it up with your income and marital money, there is a presumption that it is all now marital. There's more to it, and you can seek reimbursement, but I've always disliked this area of the law because it causes problems and trust issues in a marriage if you follow the letter of the law. This is an area where prenups and estate planning make things a lot easier and can avoid complications.

2. The Marital Home

In the beginning stages of a divorce, people frequently argue over who gets to keep the house they've put so much work into and where they raised their kids. That is, they argue until they realize they'll need to buy out their spouse's interest. After running the numbers and exploring the reality of refinancing the mortgage solely into their name and taking on more debt to buy out their spouse's half, they often change their tune. Negotiations surrounding the family home can be difficult. People are attached to their home. Some want it out of spite, others want to maintain stability for the kids. But regardless of the reason, this decision needs to be made from an investment, economic, and educated point of view.

The first thing you need to do is approximate the value of your home. To do this properly, take the fair market value of the house (what it will sell for) and deduct all the loans against it (what you owe), which will give you the equity you have in your home. The most common way to determine the fair market value is to get an appraisal, which will cost a few hundred dollars. My recommendation is to also pay for a home inspection, so you know if there are any major problems or repairs that should be factored into the total cost, and possibly fixed, before taking sole responsibility and liability for the home. Another option is to have a real estate agent run a comparative market analysis, at little to no cost, to determine what similar houses in your area are being sold for, but that is not as official and doesn't account for repairs the house may need. From there, you will be able to calculate the equity and determine how you can, or if you want to, buy out your spouse. When weighing your options, you need to consider if this will leave you in a tough position financially and if it's a wise investment to buy out your spouse's half.

Don't wait to deal with the house. It's easier to address unexpected issues before or during the process, and you can't go back on your deal after the ink is dry. If you go online, any one of the popular home listing sites will give you a good idea of what your house might be worth and with the latest mortgage statement you can run a quick ballpark of what it may be valued at. From there, you can update your one-page balance sheet for discussion with your spouse. At your initial discussions, I would recommend that you simply ask how they would like to deal with the house and agree that you both will be involved in exploring your options to see what is feasible. After getting buy-in from your spouse, I would highly recommend researching whether you have a Certified Divorce Lending Professional in your area. In the past few years, this new specialty and designation of mortgage brokers has become popular. If you find one, for no additional fee they can assist you and your spouse with evaluating who may qualify to refinance the loan, and they are extremely knowledgeable and familiar with all the options available for dealing with a house in the mist of divorce. You can also consult with an attorney, mediator, or real estate agent, and they can help you generate options and determine if you wish to remain in the house or if it may be wiser to sell.

3. Personal Property

It is a waste of resources to spend time arguing over electronics and furniture. Generally, each spouse should get 50 percent of the garage sale value of personal property. Please don't pay attorneys to discuss who gets the furniture. You could buy ten sets for what you will spend discussing it. So, in order to avoid wasting time or money arguing over your stuff, make a list of everything you own, and go item by item, choosing who will receive what and trying to make it as fair as possible. It's not worth fighting over. You can always replace things, and you won't remember who got what ten years from now. Also, please remember not to be vindictive. You both know what items have sentimental value and mean more to the other person.

When I was in court litigating divorces, I was often amazed at the lengths people would go to and the amount of attorney's fees they were willing to spend to ensure they'd get the Christmas ornaments, family photo albums, wedding china, their favorite piece of furniture, or a specific piece of art. My recommendation is always to go through every room of your house and make a spreadsheet of every single thing of value, categorized by location. If you have the time, make a thorough list because it will save you headaches and arguments down the road when you're packing up the toaster or silverware. In the spreadsheet, create three columns titled "Description of the item," "Spouse A," and "Spouse B." Go ahead and fill in any items that are your or your spouse's non-marital property, but leave the rest blank. Before checking off all the items on your wish list, I recommend giving this list to your spouse and politely asking them to add any items that you may have missed, and to put an X in their column for anything they really want to keep. From there, you can try to negotiate a fair and equal division of all your stuff, or what we call "personal property." If you run into any disagreements, table the issue for further discussion with a professional. But if you can reach an agreement on everything, congratulate yourselves for saving a ton of money and time instead of haggling over things through the lawyers at hundreds of dollars an hour.

ATTORNEY'S FEES

You only have one pot of money that makes up the marital estate. Whether you realize it or not, you and your spouse are both paying for the other's attorney. Lawyers bill by the hour, and the more work that needs to be done, the more money they make. If you understand the legal concepts, your options, and how to prepare, you can save a great deal of time and money navigating the legalities of divorce. Just remember, every penny that you or your spouse spends on an attorney could have been divided between the two of you and used for your kids' college education or a much-needed vacation.

CHAPTER 12

WEIGHING YOUR LEGAL OPTIONS FOR DIVORCE

Everything can be taken from a man but one thing: the last of the human freedoms—to choose one's attitude in any given set of circumstances, to choose one's own way.

—VIKTOR E. FRANKL, *MAN'S SEARCH FOR MEANING*

If you are contemplating divorce, it is extremely important that you are aware of your options and carefully evaluate all of them before deciding how to proceed. The right option for your family will depend on your goals, ability to cooperate and communicate, and how much input (control) each of you want over the process, cost, speed, duration, and level of privacy.

Just remember, you are only 50 percent of the equation and cannot make this decision on your own. If you have invested the time and effort to properly prepare and have done the work, you should be able to have difficult discussions and evaluate your options with your spouse at the kitchen table, or with the assistance of a professional. The legal options you need to consider are whether you want do it yourself, litigate, mediate, or collaborate.

DO IT YOURSELF

In theory, you don't need attorneys to get divorced. If you have the time and ability to negotiate an agreement, prepare the necessary documents, and navigate the court system without assistance, it is possible. Your county most likely has standardized forms that can be completed, but it's risky. Personally, I'd only recommend this option for people who don't have kids, a home, or any significant assets. Without the guidance of an attorney, you risk damaging your relationship during negotiations, spending a great deal of time completing complex paperwork, overlooking critical requirements, and spending months failing to properly navigate the court system. In theory, anyone can repair their own car or home as well, but it may not be worth the time and risk of damage when you can hire a professional who has the knowledge, experience, and ability to do an extremely important and complex job the right way, quickly and efficiently.

The risk you run in the DIY approach is that if everything is not truly agreed on in advance, or if the agreement is unfair, you may find yourself in litigation when that isn't what you intended. So, if that option interests you, you need a backup plan and a secondary approach that you've agreed upon in advance if things should go south.

If this interests you and you can negotiate effectively with your spouse, there is a hybrid DIY approach to consider. The DIY approach can be as simple as you and your spouse hiring attorneys in an advisory role. To be clear, one attorney is not allowed to represent both spouses, but if you and your spouse can realistically prepare and do the work in a healthy manner, you can have one attorney guide you through the process in what we would refer to as an uncontested divorce. Other attorneys may refer to this approach as a cooperative divorce.

My recommendation for handling this approach is that both spouses interview and meet with an attorney to educate you on the law, the legal standards where you live, and what you think is a fair resolution to your case. I would also recommend finding an attorney who is both a mediator and collaborative attorney. Furthermore, I strongly advise that both spouses take part in the initial meeting and consultation so you both hear the same information and get to make your independent judgment on whether you want to work with that attorney. Once you agree on someone to work with, set some ground rules so that you both feel comfortable with the arrangement. One spouse will then hire them as their attorney so that they can help you negotiate any issues you may have not considered and prepare all the legal documents you'll need to finalize your divorce. The other spouse will then have the option of representing themselves or hiring an attorney for two hours of their time, one to read the legal documents that have been prepared and the other to meet and advise them on their legal rights and whether the agreement is written fairly.

This is the cheapest and most efficient option to get divorced, but only a small fraction of people are ideal candidates because it requires healthy communication and an ability to negotiate a majority, if not all, of the issues directly with your spouse.

LITIGATE

Litigation is defined as "the process of taking legal action." By definition, it is an adversarial process where both spouses hire an attorney and bring their case before a court to resolve their dispute for them. From day one of your case, your attorney is required to begin preparing for trial and take the procedural steps to do so, even though more than 90 percent of divorce cases settle without going to trial. This leads to a great deal of time and resources being spent on procedural legal requirements, as opposed to focusing on settlement and working toward reaching an agreement, which would finalize the divorce as efficiently and painlessly as possible.

Litigation works effectively for business deals gone wrong, civil disputes, injuries, and crime, but it isn't effective for families who are merely trying to resolve what is already a painful period of separation. The law, by its very nature, creates an adversarial line in the sand where there will be a winner and a loser on any particular issue. This approach works great for determining whether someone is innocent or guilty of a crime or caused an accident, but when it comes to families facing divorce, no one wins. After a long, difficult legal war, both spouses will inevitably lose, and there's a large legal bill that comes along with it.

It is imperative to understand that the goal of litigation is for each attorney to get their client the best possible result, often at the expense of their opponent. So, even when you "win" on an issue, you do so at a great financial and emotional cost to your family. This whole process plays out in public and will live on for eternity in the court record. You can get copies of any court documents and all the juicy accusations against spouses in a divorce relatively easily online or at your local county clerk's office. This includes your favorite celebrities, your family members, and friends—and one day your children will be able to get yours.

During litigation, typically all negotiations will go through the attorneys, and communicating with your spouse is not encouraged. This reduces the interaction of the parties and their ability to communicate in a productive or healthy manner. Over time, the lack of communication allows their minds to wander, and they often begin to assume the worst about their spouse's intentions and become hostile toward one another. As the case drags on, they become more reliant on their attorneys to address disagreements, which leads to additional litigation related to their children after the divorce. Lawyers refer to this as post-decree litigation, and I can easily recall a few dozen clients who went through a difficult divorce and then would come back to me, year after year, with a new issue to fight about in court. The amount that they spent was shocking. For lawyers, these couples effectively become an annuity for their business that they can count on to bring in anywhere from $5,000 to $20,000 in revenue each year. It's a sad reality and I always did my best to repair the underlying issues and encourage my clients to resolve their case through reasonable settlement proposals. Unfortunately, we were only half of the equation and powerless to end the case without a reasonable and willing negotiating partner, which often led to unnecessary, lengthy, and expensive legal battles.

MEDIATE

When someone first calls my office looking for a healthier approach to divorce, the only process and word that people seem to know to ask for is "mediation." But most aren't aware of what mediation is or how it differs from the other options. So, to clear up any confusion: Mediation is a voluntary, private, and confidential process in which a neutral and impartial person assists the parties in negotiating their differences. A mediator goes through training to get certified in interest-based negotiation. There are several approaches to mediation, and I won't bore you with the formal legalese and describe the differences between facilitative, evaluative, or transformative mediation. All you need to know is that the most common form of mediation is where the mediator does not decide what is fair or right, assess blame, give advice, or render an opinion. Typically, they remain in a neutral role, where the decision-making power is left strictly up to the parties. Some mediators, when asked, will render an opinion, but most will avoid picking sides or making a final recommendation unless pushed to do so.

Mediation can save you time and money, encourage increased involvement of the parties, and allow for creative solutions. The goal of mediation is to separate the people from the problem, focus on interests instead of positions, generate options for mutual gain, and allow the parties to come to a mutual agreement. For mediation to be successful, it requires a commitment from both parties, because it's voluntary, and either party can terminate the process at any time. In divorce mediation, once you come to an agreement, the mediator is not permitted to act on either party's behalf. So, you will typically receive a memorandum outlining your agreement and then the mediator will give you a few recommendations for attorneys. You and your spouse will have to interview and retain attorneys to prepare the agreement and assist you in court. You should know that mediation is not binding and the memorandum is not a final, signed agreement. So, if your spouse later decides they don't like the terms agreed upon in mediation, they can back out. So don't delay; get your agreement signed and entered in court as quickly as possible. In addition, be very careful when selecting an attorney to prepare and review the agreement following mediation. The last thing you want is to derail your agreement or cause unnecessary conflict after investing the time and money to go through a full mediation process. Once again, I'd recommend using attorneys trained in collaborative law and who have a good working relationship with your mediator so your agreement will be honored.

COLLABORATE

This is the ideal option for parents and their children. A collaborative divorce is a private, confidential, and nonadversarial process. Both parties hire their own attorneys and any other experts they choose. The lawyers and experts must be trained and certified as mediators and collaborative practitioners. Everyone refers to themselves as a member of the "team," and signs a contract requiring them to settle the case without going to court (a Participation Agreement). The concept is a settlement-only approach, conducted outside of the court system, where everyone is required to act in a transparent, honest, and cooperative manner to resolve the entire case in private and behind closed doors. All negotiations take place in meetings that are focused on modeling healthy dispute resolution. The professionals (attorneys and experts) help prepare the couple for team meetings. It's still a divorce and never a bed of roses, but the team meetings allow families to speak freely and work through issues privately, which allows couples to have open discussions and typically helps to avoid the negative financial and emotional consequences of divorce.

Commitment to a collaborative divorce requires that if the process fails, your lawyers will have to withdraw, and the case will need to be handed over to trial lawyers to litigate in court. Although this may sound harsh or unappealing, it is actually what makes this option successful; it removes the threat of going to court and no one wants to start over and end up in front of a judge after investing so much time and effort.

The collaborative process differs from mediation, because each party has their own active counsel to privately assist them. They will offer an opinion on a fair resolution and assist in helping you to negotiate a reasonable, fair, and agreed upon resolution to your case. They do this while ensuring that your wishes and opinions are considered throughout the process. Your team will support you at every stage of the journey, and you won't have to hire anyone else because they will oversee the case from start to finish.

The real benefit of a collaborative divorce is that you can decide to bring in team members with their own expertise to assist in various roles. For example, a therapist (or family specialist) with education and experience in child development can assist your family in negotiating the parenting issues and help your kids through the process. A financial neutral can collect all your financial records and assist you and your spouse with any budgeting, tax, financial, and retirement planning issues you may have. A tax expert might analyze the impact of a hyper-technical and important tax issue to save your family a great deal of money upon divorce or on either of your deaths. A neutral expert can be brought in to assist with any specific task that may be needed, from valuing a business or a piece of art to securing life insurance. The team can be as big or as small as you want, but my experience is that this division of responsibilities works out to be much more efficient and cost-effective because it allows the lawyers to focus on legal issues. Other members of the team concentrate on their select roles at a fraction of the cost of an attorney, who would typically fulfill all these roles during litigation. Having seen firsthand how parenting issues can cause two to three years of litigation, it's amazing to witness how parents attend two meetings with a family specialist and resolve all their parenting issues peacefully in thirty to sixty days.

A collaborative divorce is generally less expensive and much quicker than litigation. It encourages healthy communication, keeps children out of the controversy and helps couples maintain their integrity, respect, dignity, and privacy throughout the process. Collaboration can go at whatever pace the couple wishes, avoids all procedural requirements mandated in court, and allows for much greater flexibility and creative problem-solving. Like mediation, it requires a commitment from both parties to the process and helps them civilly resolve their divorce in a strategic, smart, and healthy manner.

CHAPTER 13

WHAT YOU'RE IN FOR

Any change, even a change for the better, is always accompanied by drawbacks and discomforts.

—ARNOLD BENNETT

In the previous chapters, we've covered how to prepare for a successful divorce, the legal issues you need to be aware of, and the various options available to you for dissolving the marriage. Now I want to give you a brief overview of what you're in for as you navigate the process and the critical stages you'll encounter.

THE STAGES OF DIVORCE

There are eight phases of divorce. Depending on the model, approach, and legal choices you make, each option will have a very different impact on you, your family, and your bank account.

1. Selecting the Process

Not everyone is a candidate for all the options we covered in the previous chapter (DIY, litigate, mediate, collaborate). Sometimes litigation is necessary even though it may be not ideal. As the co-founder of a nonprofit that assists survivors with leaving abusive marriages, I acknowledge that there are dire circumstances in which litigation is the only option to protect the safety and well-being of the parties and children. Correspondingly, a collaborative divorce is not only for couples who are skipping down the street, holding hands and singing "Kumbaya." We can achieve successful results with the collaborative process in extremely difficult and complex cases by bringing in team members to assist and manage high-conflict and emotionally charged issues involving finances, mental health, or addiction. These complicated and highly sensitive issues can be delicately discussed and addressed in a private setting, openly and honestly, instead of simply being weaponized, denied, or ignored in court. That's why it's important to take your time and interview several attorneys and mediators to discover which approach may be the best fit for your family.

I've been involved in collaborative and mediation cases where people suffering from sex and substance addiction acknowledge their issues in meetings, apologize to their spouse, work through their issues together, and develop trust over time. While apologizing, they also agree to reimburse their spouse for any money they spent as a result of their problematic behavior during the marriage, which is totaled up and accounted for by the financial neutral. *This never happens in litigation.* There's no apology or acknowledgement of fault. You simply enter into years of accusations and fighting to prove (or disprove) what both spouses already know to be the truth. In the end, because they never come clean and admit their wrongdoing, it ends up bankrupting their family financially and emotionally, causing damage that often can never be repaired.

On the other hand, I've also had collaborative cases where one spouse is so paranoid and distrusting that they are never going to agree to anything without a judge weighing in to make the final decision. In other collaborative cases, I've had parties take completely unreasonable positions and try to strong-arm the other party into an unfair deal. I've also had cases where one party simply refuses to participate after not getting what they want. In these cases, litigation may be the only answer. The key is to spot these issues as quickly as possible and identify when people are no longer candidates for an out-of-court resolution to their divorce. If you allow one party to drag things out longer than necessary and don't shut these tactics down quickly, it becomes a waste of time and money for everyone involved.

The most common problem I come across is couples who are trying to save money. Sometimes, clients trick themselves into believing they're candidates for an uncontested or cooperative divorce. They think it will be cheaper to stay out of court or to only use one attorney to try to settle the case, but these options require the parties to cooperate and compromise. If a couple can't stand to be in the same room or agree on what color the sky is at any given moment, it's highly unlikely they're capable of civilly negotiating an agreement. Don't get me wrong, I've settled quite a few of these cases outside of court. While it may not have been pretty and tensions ran high, they came to an agreement with the support of a good team of professionals.

The other misguided money-saving mistake is when couples opt to not add a necessary member to the team, like a coach, financial neutral, or child specialist, because they don't think they "need" them and can work these things out themselves. In the end, the couple would have saved time, money, and a great deal of stress by bringing in an expert to assist and support them when navigating these challenging and highly personal issues.

An option that fits the dynamic of one family may not work for another. The right choice for your family often boils down to how well you can communicate, if you both can be somewhat reasonable, are willing to negotiate somewhat fairly, and you can come to an agreement on these difficult issues with your spouse. That's why you shouldn't rush into a decision until you've seriously evaluated each of your options (and hopefully, discussed them with your spouse so you're on the same page).

2. Selecting Attorneys

The attorneys you and your spouse select will dictate the options that are available to you. Lawyers want your business, and collaborative law is still a new concept. Most attorneys and judges are still not familiar with these out-of-court alternatives nor are they trained to handle them. You may find that you are being steered away from collaborative law and toward litigation by well-meaning but uninformed professionals. They want your business, as do all attorneys, but the offer and model are drastically different, along with how they will affect your family's future. So if you are considering a collaborative divorce or mediation, you will have to seek out a lawyer who is trained and specializes in those areas.

The traditional process of selecting attorneys is that each spouse independently interviews and hires counsel without consulting or involving the other. It may sound odd and unorthodox, but in mediation or collaborative, you may interview potential attorneys jointly as a couple. If it makes you feel more comfortable, or if there are highly sensitive issues that you need to discuss confidentially, you can interview a mediator or collaborative attorney independently. Regardless of how you approach this stage, it's always helpful to discuss what happens with your spouse, compare notes, and help educate each other on what you've learned, your goals, and what you hope to achieve throughout the process. I realize this may not be comfortable for most, but at a minimum, a simple email between spouses will suffice. If you can't bear to have this conversation directly, a few marriage counseling sessions with an experienced therapist who is trained in collaborative law may be a good idea.

Just so you are aware: If you choose to mediate, the mediator will most likely recommend attorneys who they have worked with and who can quickly and amicably finalize your agreement. If you choose to collaborate, it's ideal to coordinate and hire two attorneys who are familiar with each other and enjoy working together. It will result in a much more comfortable, efficient, and smooth process. Regardless of the option that you choose, attorneys who support your goals and work well together will be capable of settling your case much faster and at a lower cost.

3. Starting the Case

In litigation, the first thing your attorney will do is prepare a petition for you to sign that is filed with the court. Once it's filed, in most counties, a case number is generated, a judge is assigned, and your first court date is automatically scheduled. Your attorney is then required to give notice to your spouse. Depending on your attorney's approach, they will either write a letter to your spouse introducing themselves and asking them to "waive service," or they will hire someone to serve your spouse with the petition. Process servers typically serve people at home, at their office, or in public. This step alone can set the tone for your entire case and start you down a path that you never intended or wanted. If your spouse isn't aware the petition is coming, or if they're served in public, it can cause embarrassment, fear, or anger. The documents will look very official and specify formal deadlines, which may cause additional anxiety and urgency. What's more, the standard language in the petition your attorney had you sign will often offend your spouse. They may assume the worst about your intentions based on the legal jargon and what your attorney told you is required to be in the document. Trust me, it isn't a healthy way to start an already difficult process, based on the frantic and irate calls I regularly received after people were served.

After your spouse is served, they'll hire an attorney and formally respond to your petition. Each attorney will then independently work with you and your spouse to begin fulfilling their legal obligations in preparation for the first court date and reporting their progress to the judge. The first court date will typically occur several months after the petition is filed. During these first few months of litigation, you and your spouse will spend thousands of dollars in attorney's fees without moving you much closer to a resolution.

In mediation and collaborative, there are no standard requirements or a one-size-fits-all approach to begin your case. You are truly in control of the process. Regardless of whether you interview attorneys jointly, hire an attorney independently, break the news to your spouse yourself, or let your attorney do it for you, the process allows for much greater flexibility. There is no paperwork filed in court and the beginning of the case will be based on your comfort level. If you are comfortable discussing your options and how you want to proceed with your spouse directly, great, please do so. If you aren't comfortable, your mediator/attorney can provide you with materials to give to your spouse to review, or they can write your spouse a nice letter to explain the benefits.

Once the attorney(s) has been hired for mediation, collaborative, or an uncontested case, you will formally start the process by booking an initial meeting. At that meeting, the attorney(s) will go over the ground rules, discuss how you want to proceed, your goals, concerns, and immediately begin to address the issues in your case. The process is informal and directly focused on moving your case forward. The first meeting will typically happen within a few weeks of hiring your attorneys or mediator.

4. Temporary Issues

At the beginning of your case, there will likely be a few issues that need to be resolved quickly. You may need to determine living arrangements, how the bills are going to get paid and where paychecks are going to be deposited, establish temporary support payments, or work out a parenting schedule.

In litigation, for each of the temporary issues that need to be addressed, the attorneys will once again prepare one or more petitions for you to sign and file them with the court. The attorneys will then appear in court to present each petition. Depending on your local courthouse, it can take anywhere from several weeks to several months to get a court date, and at that court date, your spouse's attorney will be granted time to prepare and file a response. This process typically requires a minimum of two to three court dates before a decision will be made, and depending on the issues and the court's schedule, the process for one petition to be resolved can take anywhere from two months to more than a year, depending on the issue, the county, and the courtroom. In the meantime, your attorneys may or may not be able to negotiate an agreement between the two of you. If they don't, you will be required to appear in court and testify in a hearing. All of this will cost you significant amounts in attorney's fees, and it damages your ability to communicate and civilly coexist with your spouse because your attorney will draft the petition in a way that asks for the greatest possible result and makes you look good, while making your spouse look bad.

In comparison, if you choose mediation, collaborative, or an uncontested process, you can simply discuss any pressing or immediate issues that need to be addressed, evaluate a range of options to settle the issue, and reasonably resolve them at the first meeting. If you are unable to reach an agreement at that initial meeting, or if additional information is required to have a meaningful discussion, you can schedule a follow-up meeting within a short period of time.

5. Discovery

During the initial stages of your case, your attorneys will be conducting what we call "discovery." This is a fancy legal term for the process of requesting, collecting, and exchanging documents and information. In litigation, this process can be time-consuming and expensive because lawyers need to protect themselves and their clients. So they send massive formal document requests and turn over every stone imaginable, while the other side is trying to avoid disclosing as much information as possible.

These discovery requests will typically ask for years of documents, and it often takes my clients a significant amount of time to dig everything up. Each attorney is then required to collect, exchange, and review every page, most of which isn't relevant or helpful to the case. I've had responses that range from dozens of pages to tens of thousands. Typically, when going through this process, people won't turn over everything that was requested, inviting even more work, litigation, and cost. The discovery process can initiate a lengthy back-and-forth between the attorneys that spans months, if not years. The attorneys will also submit formal legal questions that you will need to answer called interrogatories. They may also take depositions, which are formal interviews in which both spouses and their attorneys are present, and a court reporter documents every word.

In mediation, collaborative, and uncontested cases, the documents to be exchanged will be discussed and agreed upon at meetings. You won't be conducting formal discovery, so only what is needed is exchanged. Meaning, if two spouses both have access to an account and feel comfortable with the finances, they only need to provide the most current statement, but if one spouse isn't familiar with the finances or a particular account, they can be given the password and online access, or years' worth of statements if they want. The point is that the clients are in full control over what is and what is not necessary, not a judge or the attorneys. Plus, if one spouse isn't as financially savvy, they can go through the documents, ask questions, and get the support of the financial neutral, if helpful.

Furthermore, unlike in litigation where both attorneys independently review and exchange both sets of documents, only one person will need to review the documents (the financial specialist or attorney) and prepare the necessary summaries to present at your meetings. These alternative options will save you a lot of time and money, and allow you to avoid all the formal legal requirements and procedures because you aren't in court and you control the process.

6. Settlement Negotiations

For each issue that arises in litigation, a petition will need to be prepared, along with a response. All negotiations will typically go through the attorneys. A settlement will either be agreed upon or the judge will decide for you after a hearing. In mediation, collaborative and uncontested cases, these issues will be addressed out in the open during meetings, with both spouses' input.

When it comes to formal settlement proposals to resolve your case, in litigation each attorney will typically prepare a proposal, review it with their client to get their approval, and then submit it to the other side. This takes time and a lot of work. Upon receiving the proposal, the other side will also review it with their client, and then either edit it or draft their own agreement from scratch. Then, they'll review that draft with their client and submit it in response. During this process, clients often have no interaction and don't directly discuss the settlement negotiations; instead, everything goes through the lawyers.

In my experience, it is rare for a settlement conference with both parties and their attorneys to occur in litigation until the case is scheduled for trial, if at all. If you find yourself in a settlement conference during litigation, it is often contentious because the lawyers do most of the talking and they're focused on impressing their client and vigorously defending them instead of attempting to listen to both parties, understanding their point of view, and coming to a reasonable agreement. Even though more than 90 percent of cases settle without a trial, far too many cases settle within days of trial, or even worse, on the day of at the courthouse. At that point, the attorneys have already done the work to prepare for going to trial, and the emotional and financial damage has been done. When this happens, and it happens in a significant percentage of cases, people are forced to make extremely important decisions very quickly and under great stress, and they often feel unprepared and overwhelmed negotiating on the fly.

With mediation, collaborative, and uncontested cases, negotiations directly involving both parties occur at every stage of the process, and you will have time to carefully consider and weigh your options. The attorneys and clients will coordinate, discuss, and agree upon who is going to prepare the settlement documents to minimize the work needed to be done. By its very nature, the process is much more efficient, cost-effective, and alleviates unnecessary work or redundancy. I have been involved in litigation cases where more than thirty drafts of formal settlement documents have been exchanged, which occurred over multiple years, and cost the parties hundreds of thousands of dollars.

In case you haven't realized by now, when it comes to family law and divorce, I am of the opinion that the litigation process is broken and simply doesn't work for families. The delay, lack of communication, and uncertainty about what the other person is thinking, doing, or scheming up causes most people to lose their minds. That, coupled with the mounting legal bills, can be a recipe for disaster when it comes to your mental health. Even the most happy-go-lucky and even-keeled clients eventually start to crack and become an unrecognizable version of themselves. The immense emotional and financial stress of divorce takes a toll on people after years of litigation. I've been a part of cases where people drank themselves to oblivion, threw away their life savings, career, and relationship with their children, and in one case, even took their own life. It's devastating and causes ripple effects throughout their family. Far too many times, I've had to stand in court and argue over police reports involving death threats, domestic violence, or children who were involuntarily committed after attempting to commit suicide, all because of this process. What I've learned is that if people can simply sit down and have a conversation, with the right professional help, in a healthy environment where they feel heard and understood, it makes all the difference. Even if they don't get the exact result they want during settlement negotiations, couples can work through difficult issues and get divorced without losing their family, wealth, and legacy in the process.

7. Time and Attorney's Fees

Mediation, collaborative law, or an uncontested approach allows your family to control the schedule, take breaks for personal reasons, accomplish necessary tasks, and experiment with possible parenting schedules or settlement options. In litigation, the judge controls the schedule and court dates will typically be scheduled every thirty to sixty days so your attorneys can report the status of the case to the court. Often nothing is accomplished at these court appearances, but your attorneys will be required to spend time preparing and going to court, which results in attorney's fees. In between these status updates, as issues arise in your case, the attorneys will be required to draft additional motions, legal briefs, and memoranda that only lead to more court dates. Ultimately, the difference between these options is that, in litigation, the attorneys will spend a great deal of time complying with their legal obligations and procedure, while in mediation, collaborative, and uncontested, the attorney's time will be spent focusing on how to meet your goals and settle your case.

Regardless of the option you choose, even under the best of circumstances divorce is not cheap. No one can predict the cost because it is completely dependent on the couple, the complexity of the issues, and their willingness to come to an agreement. Whatever the final cost, as a fair warning, it will be more expensive than you'd expect. To brace you for the impact and what to expect, when I'm asked to make a prediction, I've always told people that it can cost anywhere from $5,000 to $500,000, depending on the circumstances. Well-renowned attorneys and statisticians have estimated, based on national trends and data, that on average, the cost of divorce equals about 40 percent of a married family's annual income.[53] The best analogy that I've heard on the cost of a collaborative divorce is: "In most collaborative cases, the total costs for both attorneys, coaches, expert fees, filing fees, and so on will be less than what you'd spend to sell your house (around six to eight percent in commissions, closing costs, and so on)."[54] Keep in mind that a collaborative case should generally be much less expensive than a litigated divorce, but an uncontested case will be the cheapest option.

To illustrate this point, here are two examples of realistic legal bills for the first three months of a litigated divorce and a collaborative divorce. As you will see, both are virtually the same amount, but

---

53 "Divorce Dollars: The 10 Costliest States to End a Marriage," *Modern Salon*, last modified January 20, 2024, https://www.modernsalon.com/1089591/divorce-dollars-the-10-costliest-states-to-end-a-marriage.

54 Stuart G. Webb and Ronald D. Ousky, *The Collaborative Way to Divorce: The Revolutionary Method That Results in Less Stress, Lower Costs, and Happier Kids—Without Going to Court* (New York: Plume, 2007), 141.

in the litigated case very little has been accomplished or resolved, while the collaborative divorce is on the verge of completion. The difference:

- **Selecting the Process and Attorneys:** In the collaborative divorce, the couples have met with their attorneys together, at that initial meeting recommendations were provided for the second attorney, who was hired within one week. Conversely, it takes seven weeks for the second attorney to be retained in the litigated case.
- **Starting the Case and Temporary Issues:** In the collaborative example, a team meeting has taken place within three weeks of beginning the process, the couple has shared their goals, concerns, and all temporary issues have been resolved during the first meeting. In the litigated case, one court date has taken place, four petitions have been filed, and nothing has been resolved or addressed.
- **Settlement Negotiations and Discovery:** In first three months of the litigated divorce, no negotiations have taken place, the attorneys have exchanged requests for the production of documents ("discovery"), and four petitions have been filed making requests, but nothing has been resolved. In the collaborative example, three team meetings have taken place, the couple has met with the financial specialist and child specialist several times, all documents have been exchanged, they have generally negotiated the terms of an agreement, and the attorneys have begun preparing the initial draft settlement documents.

LITIGATED DIVORCE

INVOICE

John Doe
123 Main Street
Anywhere, IL 12345

Date: January 1 - March 31

Date	Description	Hours	Hourly Rate	Total
1/15	Initial Consultation with John Doe (1.0); Prepared Retainer Agreement (.25); Opened case file (.5). (Billing 1.75, No Charge 1.25)	.5	$450	$225.00
1/16	Draft Petition for Dissolution of Marriage (1.0); Summons (.25); E-mail to client enclosing petition for review and actions to be taken (.2); E-mail response from client approving petition (.1); Prepared petition for electronic signature (.25); Electronic Filing (.3); Received file-stamped petition, downloaded to e-file, review and created calendar event for upcoming court appearance (.25).	2.35	$450	$1,057.50
1/19	Review of file (.1); Telephone call to client re: service (.35); Draft Waiver of Service (.4); Draft Correspondence to opposing party and e-mail enclosing same (.35).	1.2	$450	$540.00
1/26	Review of file; Prepared Proof of Service, correspondence to process server and Notice of Filing; Retained process server for service.	1.15	$450	$517.50
2/3	Received correspondence from process server enclosing confirmation of Service; Draft Notice of Filing and electronic filing; E-mail to client.	.55	$450	$247.50
2/15	Telephone call from client re: case facts and petitions to prepare (.65); Draft Petition for Temporary Custody, Child Support and Maintenance (1.25); E-mail to client for review (.2).	2.1	$450	$945.00
2/16	E-mail from client re: edits (.25); Review and edits to Petitions (.55); Prepared for electronic signature (.25); Received e-mail enclosing executed petitions (.1); Prepare Notice of Motion and Proof of Service (.35); Electronically filed all documents and scheduling of court appearance (.4); Created calendar event for court appearance and e-mail to client re: same (.2); Received electronically filed petition via e-mail and downloaded to e-file (.15); E-mail to client enclosing same (.1); Prepared correspondence to opposing party enclosing same (.3).	1.85	$450	$832.50
3/2	Telephone call from opposing attorney re: retention and case facts (.6); Received correspondence enclosing NOF and Appearance, scanned and saved to e-file (.25); E-mail to client enclosing same (.1); Telephone call from client re: status and upcoming court appearance (.8).	1.75	$450	$787.50
3/5	E-mail from client enclosing financial affidavit; Review of file and legal research; Draft discovery request, interrogatories, Proof of Service and Notice of Filing; E-mail to opposing attorney and client enclosing same.	1.1	$450	$495.00
3/10	Initial Court Appearance for presentation of petitions and scheduling of hearing (1.0); Travel to and from Court Appearance (.55); Scanned Order to e-file and e-mail to client enclosing same (.3); Telephone call with client re: court appearance and actions to be taken (.6).	2.45	$450	$1,102.50
3/13	Review of file and legal research; Draft Petition to Establish Parenting Schedule (1.0); Petition to Appoint Guardian Ad Litem (1.0); E-mail to client enclosing same (.1).	2.1	$450	$945.00
3/19	In office meeting with client re: case facts, review of financial documents, discovery production and executed petitions (1.25); Draft Notice of Filing, Proof of Service and prepared for electronic filing (.6)	1.85	$450	$832.50
3/30	E-mail from client enclosing voluminous financial records; Review and organized all financial records for production; Proof of Service and NOF.	2.25	$450	$1,012.50

THANK YOU!

Total: $9,540.00

COLLABORATIVE DIVORCE

INVOICE

John Doe
123 Main Street
Anywhere, IL 12345

Date: January 1 - March 31

Date	Description	Hours	Hourly Rate	Total
1/15	Initial Consultation with Jane and John Doe (1.0); Prepared Retainer Agreement (.25); Opened case file (.5). (Billing 1.75, No Charge 1.25)	.5	$450	$225.00
1/26	Telephone call from Attorney Johnson re: retention, case facts, scheduling and preparation for initial team meeting (.6); Three (3) e-mails from and to team re: scheduling, created calendar event (.3); Telephone call to client re: preparation for same (.45).	1.35	$450	$607.50
2/2	Preparation for team meeting and draft agenda (.6); E-mail to and from Attorney Johnson re: agenda (.3); E-mail to Team enclosing Agenda (.1).	1	$450	$450.00
2/4	Initial Team Meeting (1.5); Draft Meeting Notes (.5); E-mail to Team enclosing notes and recommended professionals (.15).	2.15	$450	$967.50
2/12	E-mail from financial neutral re: retention.	.1	$450	$45.00
2/16	E-mail from child specialist re: retention; Four professionals e-mails re: status and scheduling of professionals meeting.	.4	$450	$180.00
2/20	Professionals Meeting (1.0); Telephone call to client re: preparation for upcoming team meeting and meeting with professionals (.55).	1.55	$450	$697.50
2/23	Preparation for team meeting and draft agenda (.5); Four professionals' e-mails re: agenda (.4); E-mail to Team enclosing Agenda (.1)	1	$450	$450.00
2/25	Second Team Meeting (1.75); Draft Meeting Notes (.4).	2.15	$450	$967.50
3/18	Professionals Meeting to discuss negotiations on parenting issues, review of financial summaries, budgets and support calculations; Telephone call to client in preparation for upcoming team meeting (.5)	1.5	$450	$675.00
3/20	E-mail from child specialist enclosing Memorandum of Agreement.	.35	$450	$157.50
3/24	Third Team Meeting (1.9); Draft Meeting Notes and E-mail to Team (.45)	2.35	$450	$1,057.50
3/30	Draft Parenting Agreement; E-mail to team for review in preparation for upcoming team meeting; Telephone call to client re: same.	2.75	$450	$1,237.50
3/31	Draft proposed Marital Settlement Agreement; E-mail to professionals for review and comment.	3.4	$450	$1,530.00

THANK YOU!

Total: $9,247.50

Now, these are mere examples, but also common real-life experiences that I have been through many times. As you will see in litigation, time and resources are spent on legal procedure, while in a collaborative divorce, every line item is focused on helping the parties work toward settlement.

There is no right approach for any family, and everyone is different, but it is important that you make an educated decision about how you want to proceed and how it will affect your family's finances and future. Like a house, a car, or a wedding, the best option is not usually the cheapest, and the right choice for one family will not be right for another. The question is what is best for your family.

8. Post-Divorce

The decisions you make leading up to and during a divorce will determine the future of your life. What most parents don't realize is that the end of your marriage isn't the end of your divorce. Attorneys refer to this stage of a case as "post-decree," and this part of your life will be shaped by the process that you participated in, the foundation of communication, trust, and problem-solving skills that were developed (or destroyed) during the divorce, as well as the legal issues that arise after the marriage has ended. Mediation, collaborative, and an uncontested approach can improve a couple's ability to communicate in a healthy manner, effectively negotiate, and utilize interest-based problem-solving skills post-divorce. If any issues arise post-divorce that cannot be resolved directly, they can contact their team for assistance. For instance, a financial neutral can run updated support calculations if either person receives a raise or loses their job, while a child specialist can assist the parties in addressing any parenting issues or concerns. The couple can quickly and effectively address problems and do so at a fraction of the cost because they are using the services of the specialist. Correspondingly, if a couple mediated, they can simply reengage the services of their mediator.

In my former life as a litigator, my clients would regularly ask me:

- Why is my ex-spouse allowed to continually drag me back into court year after year?
- Why am I being punished and forced to pay significant attorney's fees for issues that don't deserve the court's attention?
- Why can't I simply move on with my life?

It's a sad reality, but people are often left angry, bitter, and broke after a contentious divorce.

The court system isn't the forum to address emotional wounds or repair relationships. Post-divorce, people often use litigation to harass an ex-spouse and seek retribution for what they believe was an unfair result, or simply to continue communicating with their ex, no matter how unhealthy or costly it may be. Unfortunately, there's usually no consequence for repeatedly coming back to court post-divorce to exert what little control they still have over their ex, but it's a common reality that many couples face for years. Not only do their finances and personal lives suffer, but so do their children. Even though it's completely inappropriate, far too many couples place their children in the middle of their conflict, subjecting them to negative comments, providing them with details about the court case, and asking them to choose sides. This can have an extremely detrimental impact on the kids, leaving emotional scars that will last for the rest of their lives. In fact, as I mentioned previously, the studies show that divorce can have a more harmful effect on children than the death of a parent.

TAKE A DEEP BREATH

After decades of guiding people through the process of divorce, I understand the emotional roller coaster you'll go through leading up to and during a divorce. It's frightening, and the fear of the unknown can drive you crazy if you let it. You may be worried about the future and major changes in your life, your children's lives, your finances, and the loss of your identity as a husband, wife, father, or mother. It's natural, but if you can focus on the outcome that you want for your family, it will help you to make good choices, maintain your integrity, and focus on what is most important during difficult moments.

Just be careful of what influences you are allowing into your life and decision-making during divorce. You'll probably be getting input from the internet, family, friends, and coworkers who are divorced, and trust me, they're not the best source for legal advice, especially if they've been through a difficult divorce themselves. My experience tells me that people who have been scarred by divorce like to give others advice. It has become a part of their identity, and they love to talk about it with anyone who will listen. They think they are experts, but really, they're a real-life example of what not to do. Ask yourself: Would you take financial advice from someone who is broke or dating advice from someone who's never been in a serious relationship?

When it comes to divorce, I understand that nothing is easy. As hard as it may be, if you do the work to prepare, work on yourself, and approach your divorce with the right mindset, it will pay off. Just keep reminding yourself:

- One day you will wake up and realize that after winter, comes spring, and every ending brings a new beginning.
- Although you may be going through one of the most difficult times of your life, if you have the vision and wisdom to realize that your best days lie ahead of you, it will give you a different perspective.
- Problems can be gifts that we grow from, if we learn from them.
- What you believe may be the worst moment of your life in the present can eventually lead you to the best moments of your future and the person you were destined to become.
- The next chapter of your life will be written by you, and only you have the power to make it a magnificent one.
- Focus on the future that you want for your family twenty years from now, make good choices, and act accordingly. Life will take care of the rest.

SECTION 5

ARE YOU READY TO HIRE AN ATTORNEY?

If you find yourself in need of a lawyer, you'll likely turn to your friends and family for recommendations, while also scouring online reviews. All too often, this decision must be made quickly, at a time when you're under great pressure and stress. You're looking for answers and someone you can trust to guide you in your time of need. If you'd like to avoid financial, mental, and emotional devastation simply because you hired the wrong attorney, it's important to understand the business of law and the outcome you truly want.

CHAPTER 14

CHOOSING YOUR ATTORNEY

The first thing we do, let's kill all the lawyers.

—WILLIAM SHAKESPEARE
HENRY VI, PART 2, ACT IV, SCENE II

Litigation isn't usually the best way to solve your problems. Attorneys are obligated by the rules of professional conduct to "zealously protect and pursue their client's legitimate interests, within the bounds of the law."[55] So, not only are attorneys required to represent you vigorously, but they benefit from it.

55 American Bar Association. Model Rules of Professional Conduct: Preamble & Scope. Accessed May 2025. www.americanbar.org/groups/professional_responsibility/publications/model_rules_of_professional_conduct/model_rules_of_professional_conduct_preamble_scope.

Attorneys bill by the hour and can be incentivized to create conflict because the more time they spend addressing your problems and disagreements, the more money they make. During my career as a litigator, I saw this trend get worse year after year. That is why it is imperative that you know what to look for and what questions to ask when you are interviewing attorneys.

In the majority of my initial litigation or divorce consultations, the first questions I received from people were:

- How much is this going to cost?
- How much is my retainer going to be?
- Am I "aggressive" and up to the task of fighting for them?

For the record, these are the last questions you want to ask an attorney. If you are asking yourself why, then definitely continue reading before interviewing attorneys.

THE FIVE STEPS TO FOLLOW WHEN HIRING A LAWYER

Here is the advice I give to anyone who is starting their search for someone to hire.

1. Do Your Research

Don't rush into hiring an attorney. I realize you may have gotten served legal documents that say you have to file an answer within thirty days. As a result, you're nervous, overwhelmed, and desperate to make this problem go away as quickly as humanely possible. My advice is to take a deep breath and take your time. If you go to that first court date and tell the judge you need time to hire a lawyer, you are not getting charged attorney's fees for that court date, and your initial thirty days will become sixty or ninety days when the judge grants you a continuance. Don't procrastinate on interviewing and hiring an attorney, but it is standard that the court will grant you more time to do your research and find the right attorney, if you ask. Don't get nervous if the judge requires you to file an appearance to declare that you are representing yourself (*pro se*), just go ahead and do what they ask while you finalize your selection of the right attorney.

Just remember, things happen quickly for people who aren't accustomed to the process and verbiage used in court, so don't agree to anything or delve into a discussion regarding issues that you don't fully understand. Simply let the judge know that you have been making a good faith effort to interview and hire an attorney, then ask for more time to retain a lawyer and leave it at that. Be prepared for the judge to ask you how much time you need. No matter what happens, don't argue with the judge; simply say "thank you" and end the conversation.

Bonus Tip: If I were seeking a continuance to hire an attorney, I would politely request an additional sixty days and expect the judge to grant me thirty or forty-five.

2. Know Your Desired Outcome

If you think you want a shark—an aggressive or cut-throat trial attorney—think twice. Trial attorneys go to trial, aggressive attorneys cause conflict, and sharks try to kill anything they can, including the balance of your bank account. Do you want your case to settle quickly, cost as little as possible, and salvage any possibility of remaining friendly with your spouse, sibling, or stepparent? Or do you want to go through expensive, emotionally draining, and time-consuming litigation for years? The attorney you choose and their approach will dictate every aspect of your case. The same is true for the attorney on the other side, so it may be worth it to swallow your pride, call your spouse or family member to discuss what you've learned in this book, and for both of you to hire a mediator or settlement-focused attorneys instead.

Bonus Tip: When interviewing attorneys, provide a brief summary of your case without telling them exactly what outcome you want. Then ask:

1. If I hired you, what would your first steps be?
2. How would you approach and handle my case?
3. Based on the information available, what timeline would you reasonably expect? Or can you give me a range of how long it may take?
4. What initial retainer would you require, and what range would you estimate for the total cost?

5. What is your hourly rate and minimum billing increment?
6. Based on your experience, what outcome do you believe is most likely?

Ask follow-up questions whenever you need clarification, or want to dig deeper into their personality and how they conduct themselves in practice. Make sure you take good notes and write down each attorney's responses so you can compare them objectively and accurately.

3. Choose a Specialist

Years ago, lawyers, doctors, and other professionals had to serve in many capacities. Your local doctor delivered your children, treated you for pneumonia, and diagnosed you with a terminal illness. Your local lawyer would help you with the purchase of your home, handle your divorce, draft your estate plan, and file for bankruptcy on your behalf. They knew a little bit about a lot of subjects, but they didn't know any one of them well. As the old saying goes, "A jack-of-all-trades is a master of none." Over time, things have changed, and professionals have become specialists in all aspects of modern-day society.

When it comes to lawyers, don't hire someone who knows a little bit about a lot of things and advertises thirty different specialties on their website. Hire someone who exclusively focuses their legal practice on the outcome that you want to receive and has the expertise to guide you through making wise decisions so you can get the result you want as efficiently and cost-effectively as possible.

Bonus Tip: When interviewing attorneys, ask:

1. What areas of law do you currently practice, and what percentage of your work is devoted to each?
2. How long have you practiced in this area of law?
3. What percentage of your practice is devoted to cases like mine?
4. How frequently do you handle these cases in the county where my case will be heard?
5. Are you familiar with the judges who may be assigned to my case?
6. Based on your experience, how do those judges typically approach and resolve issues similar to mine?

It's okay if your case is not the attorney's sole practice area or if they primarily practice in your county. These questions are not intended to automatically disqualify anyone, but they will illuminate important and relevant factors to consider when comparing prospective attorneys.

4. Understand the Business of Law and Ask the Right Questions

When it comes to hiring an attorney, you need to understand that the retainer amount is a fictitious number. A retainer is not the final total, or the only payment you will make. It is simply a deposit and your initial payment to hire an attorney.

Most people who haven't worked with an attorney who bills hourly believe that a retainer, or the amount an attorney requests for payment to take the case, is a quote for the total cost to handle the case. In most cases involving death or divorce, where your attorney will be going to court on your behalf, you will be entering into what is called a "security retainer agreement."[56] What you need to understand about this agreement is that if you are hiring an attorney who is billing you by the hour, the amount you are paying is a deposit that will be applied to your bill. Personally, I've always made it a point to explain in my consultations that my clients are starting a savings account with my office, and as they receive their bill, we will draw from that savings account. But when it is depleted, they will need to replenish the amount. So, it doesn't matter if the retainer is $1,500 or $15,000, they will pay the same amount in the end. The only difference between these two attorneys is that the "more expensive" attorney, who is quoting you a higher fee, is probably being honest about the total cost of your case and doesn't want to waste their time haggling with you to pay more money down the road, while the "less expensive" attorney, quoting a lower retainer, may be inexperienced, irresponsible, or need cash quickly to pay their rent or make payroll the following week. Instead of focusing

56 Illinois Rule of Professional Conduct 1.15. www.illinoiscourts.gov/rules/supreme-court-rules?a=viii.

on the fictitious retainer amount when comparing attorneys, you want to figure out how quickly it will get depleted.

To figure that out, you need to know the hourly rate you will be charged and the time that you will be billed for. So, the questions you need to ask are:

1. What is your hourly rate?
2. What is your minimum billing increment?

The attorney should quote their hourly rate during your initial consultation. In regard to the minimum billing increment, you need to understand how lawyers bill. If you take an hour and divide it by 10, it breaks down into six-minute increments. In attorney-speak, six minutes are a .1 (or "point one"), twelve minutes is a .2, and so on. For me, personally, I've always had a .1 minimum billing increment, which is the lowest amount that you'll find. Most attorneys are using a minimum billing increment of .2 or .25 these days.

Be aware that when attorneys enter their billing, they always round up, so if you call and are on the phone for seven minutes, it becomes a .2 and gets rounded up to twelve minutes. In those cases, I always billed a .2 and discounted it by .1, because it seems unfair to charge people that way. But I know of several law firms that charge a .5 minimum billing entry. They need to pay for their 2 a.m. commercials with a snappy jingle, their billboards, and high-rise offices downtown. So what that means for you in real life application is: If you send them a two-sentence email that takes all of three minutes to read, they bill you for thirty minutes (a .5 minimum entry). Then they respond to your email for four minutes and schedule your next call in their calendar, which results in a bill for another thirty minutes. So, what took all of seven minutes has now resulted in an hour of billing because there were two separate tasks that were each billed at a minimum billing entry of .5. Don't fall for this, and don't hire that lawyer, regardless of their retainer amount, experience, or likability. Instead, hire a lawyer who charges you fairly and takes the extra time to explain the business side of the agreement you are entering into before you hire them.

Just to illustrate what a difference the minimum billing increment can have, I've included two sample bills for an attorney, one using a .5 minimum and the other a .1 minimum.

Naturally, the time entries and illustration of minutes wouldn't be written this way on an actual bill because clients wouldn't put up with overpaying their attorney if it were that obvious. I only hope that by understanding these two basic concepts of the business of law and seeing a simple depiction of how they impact the bottom line, you'll never look at a legal bill the same way again. Just realize that if you call your attorney to *(politely and graciously)* discuss the legal bill *(shortly after receiving it)*, they should bend over backward to answer all your questions and adjust any errors.

Thankfully, none of this will apply to estate planning because you'll most likely pay a flat fee and the quote is the final charge, so you'll never see a billing statement.

Minimum Billing Increment of .1 Attorney Hourly Rate $500 (Total Time Actually Spent on Case 3 Hours 43 Minutes)		
Billable Description	**Billable Hours**	**Subtotal**
Receive & Review Email from Client (3 mins)	0.1	$50.00
Email Response to Client (5 mins)	0.1	$50.00
Attorney Draft & Review of Petition (1 hrs 5 mins)	1.1	$1,100.00
Telephone Conversation with Client (10 Mins)	0.2	$100.00
Court Appearance & Travel Time (2 hrs 10 mins)	2.2	$550.00
Scan Court Order & Save to E-File (5 mins)	0.1	$50.00
Draft & Send Email to Client Attaching Court Order (5 mins)	0.1	$50.00
Total Bill	**3.9**	**$1,950.00**

Minimum Billing Increment of .5 Attorney Hourly Rate $500 (Total Time Actually Spent on Case 3 Hours 43 Minutes)		
Billable Description	**Billable Hours**	**Subtotal**
Receive & Review Email from Client (3 mins)	0.5	$250.00
Email Response to Client (5 mins)	0.5	$250.00
Attorney Draft & Review of Petition (1 hr 5 mins)	1.5	$1,250.00
Telephone Conversation with Client (10 Mins)	0.5	$250.00
Court Appearance & Travel Time (2 hrs 10 mins)	2.5	$750.00
Scan Court Order & Save to E-File (5 mins)	0.5	$250.00
Draft & Send Email to Client Attaching Court Order (5 mins)	0.5	$250.00
Total Bill	**6.5**	**$3,250.00**

5. Ask About Values and Goals

My mom always said:

- If something sounds too good to be true, it probably is.
- You get what you pay for.
- What you ask for, you will receive.

It was good advice. So, before you hire a lawyer, take some time and ask yourself what you really want. What do you want your life to look like in twenty years? What do you want your kids' weddings, family reunions, and birthday parties to feel like after a nasty court battle with your ex or siblings? If you want to hire an aggressive attorney or a shark, please do. Sometimes it is necessary, and I refer people to my friends who like to fight all the time. But if you are reading these words, you still have a choice, and you now understand the repercussions of hiring a litigator versus a settlement-focused attorney. So, please ask yourself what you want and what you are getting yourself into before it's too late.

Additionally, have you interviewed several lawyers, and is one of them making promises that aren't consistent with the others or that sound too good to be true? If so, you may want to pause, do your research, and consider whether that lawyer is being honest with you or if they are making promises that they won't be able to live up to. Our reputation in the legal profession precedes us, and everyone is aware of the stereotypical, dishonest, bloodsucking lawyer. Hundreds of years of lawyer jokes and satire dating back to Shakespeare must have a grain of truth to them.

You also need to think long and hard about whether you really want the cheapest attorney possible. You get what you pay for. So, when weighing your options on who to hire, don't forget to factor in your goals, values, and the ultimate outcome that you want to achieve. Ask whether the attorney's approach is aligned with what you truly want.

Then, please ask yourself: How much is your future, your legacy, your. children's well-being, and their last memories of you worth? Think about how hiring the cheapest lawyer may impact your future and what matters most to you.

SELECTING AN ESTATE PLANNING ATTORNEY

Now that we've covered selecting a litigation attorney for divorce or a contested probate, let's discuss what you need to know about the selection of an estate planning attorney. When it comes to estate planning, as you already know, I'm not the biggest fan of Will planning. Probate lawyers will disagree and tell you that having a Trust is unnecessary, that it's too expensive, you live in a probate-friendly state, and they'll give you all sorts of explanations as to why you don't need a Trust. Regardless of their reasoning, please understand that where there is a Will, there is a probate, and probate lawyers like Wills because they make their living doing probate cases. I'm not being disparaging, but it's a simple fact that an attorney will make more money in a probate case than they will administering a Trust. This is especially true if your family fights over your final wishes. If your family is forced to go to court and go through probate, there is a much higher probability that they *will* fight (no pun intended).

As you now know, attorneys are incentivized to cause conflict, and if a family member is upset and wants to air their grievances, it makes it extremely easy for them to escalate the situation in court. If they interview and hire an attorney to "assert their rights," highly sensitive, internal family arguments may play out in a courtroom for months if not years. These issues could easily have been resolved in a conference room in a heated meeting that lasts less than an hour with the assistance of a trust administration attorney or a mediator.

My advice is to hire an estate planning attorney that you feel has your family's best interests at heart. They need to specialize in estate planning and stay up-to-date on the quickly changing laws and regulations of your state, the federal government, and the IRS. They also need to have systems and processes to ensure that your estate plan will be properly funded, managed, and reviewed over time so your plan will work for your family when they need it most. If they go above and beyond and implement additional services to address the intangibles that are often overlooked, such as inventorying your assets, managing your passwords, addressing your personal property, or designing the legacy that you'll leave behind through videos or letters, even better!

So, once again, you need to ask yourself if you're looking for the cheapest plan possible, or if you'd rather invest in a comprehensive plan that is slightly more expensive. Regardless of whether you end up creating a Will plan or a Trust plan, if you find the right attorney, they can help keep your family out of court and out of conflict. In the end, you may be able to significantly reduce the attorney's fees for your family and make things much easier for them at a time when they want to grieve your death, not go to court.

As Honest Abe said, "Discourage litigation. Persuade your neighbors to compromise whenever you can...Point out to them how the nominal winner is often a real loser—in fees, expenses, and waste of time. As a peacemaker, the lawyer has a superior opportunity of being a good man. There will still be business enough."[57] Those words hang on the wall of my office, and I try to live by them every day.

In my practice, I always tell my clients that I am giving them the same advice that I would give to my own family and friends. I believe that if I treat people right and charge them fairly, I'll reap the rewards tenfold in the long run. I sleep great at night knowing my clients trust me implicitly and sing my praises to others. And I do hope, as you read through this book, that it's become clear my goal is to provide introductory advice that allows you, your family, and your friends to apply the knowledge that has taken me decades to acquire so you can avoid some of life's most common legal problems.

---

57 *The Collected Works of Abraham Lincoln*, edited by Roy P. Basler, Volume II: Notes for a Law Lecture (July 1, 1850), p. 81.

SECTION 6

WHEN LIFE HAPPENS

If you have made it this far, then you have already done what most people never take the time to do. You have honestly considered some of life's most uncomfortable possibilities. Most people avoid these issues until they have no choice. They wait, procrastinate, and assume they will deal with them later, until life happens and the people they love are left to sort through the consequences.

That does not have to be your story.

While life is good and you still have options, the people you love can benefit from your preparation, wisdom, and foresight. The decisions you make today can protect them from unnecessary pain, confusion, conflict, and regret tomorrow.

This book began with a simple premise: life happens, whether we are ready or not. Marriage, divorce, disability, death, finances, parenting, court battles, family conflict, and legacy are not separate issues. They are connected parts of the same life, and the decisions you make in one area often affect everything else.

That is the heart of this book. It is not about fear. It is a legal instruction manual on how to prove your family with an example of love, responsibility, and preparation. It is about making thoughtful decisions while you are healthy, clear-minded, and in control, so the people you care about are not left guessing later. You do not need to know every answer, and you do not need to become an expert in the law. But you do need to know enough to ask better questions, choose the right guide, and take the next right step.

Life will happen. The question is whether your family will be left reacting to it and cleaning up the mess you left behind, or whether you will have taken the time to prepare them for it and set future generations of your family up for success.

Preparation is not something you do because you expect the worst. You do it because your family deserves your best.

CHAPTER 15

YOU ARE READY

Leave nothing for tomorrow which can be done today.

—ABRAHAM LINCOLN

Imagine that when you are eighteen, your parents make you go see their lawyer. In a one-hour meeting, the lawyer generally outlines your parents' plan and then kicks them out of the meeting to speak with you one-on-one. The attorney then asks you questions about your life, your family, your future, and your goals. They explain some legal concepts and ask who you want to have make financial and medical decisions for you if something happens. They share a few gems of valuable advice about insurance, finances, and setting yourself up for success while you're young. You take the advice to heart, sign a few basic estate planning documents, and hire their recommendations for a financial adviser and a life insurance agent. When you decide to get married, you visit the lawyer again with your fiancé to discuss your future and marriage goals. The attorney helps you get a premarital agreement in place. A few years later, when you are expecting your first child, you reach out to the lawyer's office to create a Trust and a Children's Protection Plan for your growing family.

Years later, after your father passes away, there are no court dates and everything seamlessly passes to your mother as the joint owner, beneficiary, and trustee of all their property. When your mother passes several years after that, the same attorney's office works hand in hand with her financial and insurance advisers to help you wind down her estate. They guide you through what to do as the trustee of your parents' Trust. Once again, there are no court dates, and everything is handled comfortably and calmly in their office. When your siblings have questions, you schedule a meeting with the lawyer, and in one meeting you all come to an agreement about how to divide up your parents' property.

It's comforting and reassuring to know that you have a trusted adviser to turn to whenever legal issues arise concerning death, disability, or divorce. It feels as if your attorney, their associates, and their employees have all become friends of the family who truly care.

It is my hope that you choose to hire an attorney who offers you this level of support because this is how I believe every attorney-client relationship should be. That is why at Family, Wealth, and Legacy Legal Solutions (FWLLS), we strive to create this white-glove experience for our clients. Life will happen and we are here for you when it does.

AND NOW, THE END IS NEAR

This book was never intended to turn you into a lawyer or to overwhelm you with legal information. Each of the legal subjects we've addressed in this book are extremely complex and require decades of experience and study to truly comprehend. The good news is that you don't need to be an expert. That's what lawyers are for. But it is extremely important for you to know your options, what questions to ask, and how to protect yourself. You need a guide, someone who is knowledgeable, trustworthy, and has your best interest in mind when you are attempting to navigate these complex areas of the law.

Writing this book was my first major step on the road to becoming that guide. This project was time-consuming and a labor of love. My wife and staff have already forbidden me from writing another. Yet, I felt that it was extremely important to educate and empower you to anticipate and avoid life's most common legal problems. Over the course of my career, I have seen far too much pain and the financial, emotional, and moral destruction of families at the hands of an adversarial legal system. Even worse, I have witnessed the long-lasting effects and the toll it takes on innocent children when they are forced to endure the tragedies I've outlined in this book. It's heartbreaking, and I quit litigating because I can no longer be a part of the problem, perpetuating conflict in a broken legal system. I realized that it didn't represent my values or how I wanted to conduct my life. My legal practice and commitment to my clients are now focused solely on providing solutions to prevent potential problems before the damage has ever been done.

I truly appreciate that you've taken this journey with me, and I would love to hear from you if you found any of this information valuable or if it helped improve your life in any way by leaving a review of this book online or on our firm website. My practice is located in Illinois, and if you're an Illinois resident and would like assistance with your legal matters, or recommendations for an attorney that you can trust in any area of the law, I'm happy to help. If you are located in any of the other forty-nine great states, please feel free to continue your journey with my office and visit www.fwlls.com, where we will regularly be publishing articles, resources, and helpful guides on many of the legal subjects we've covered throughout this book. In addition, it would be my pleasure to conduct a consult or coach you on any of the subjects contained in this book, help find you an attorney in your area, or answer any questions about the legal issues that may have caused you to take this journey with me.

Just remember: Life Happens! And when it does, I want you to be prepared and ready for anything—your Family, Wealth & Legacy deserve nothing less.

ACKNOWLEDGMENTS

First, I would like to thank and acknowledge you, the reader. If you are anything like me and your neurosis requires you to read each and every line of a book from cover to cover, I would like to take this opportunity to thank you. We live in a world where time is our greatest commodity and is the only resource which cannot be replaced. If you've entrusted me with your time, I do not take that responsibility lightly and hope the practical knowledge and actionable strategies outlined in this book will help you, your family, and loved ones for generations to come.

I also must thank all my past clients for placing their trust and faith in me to represent them through some of the darkest and most difficult times of their lives. I am eternally grateful, and it was my honor to stand alongside, support, and defend them. It was their pain, anxiety, trauma, unimaginable stress, and grief that inspired the contents of this book. Sharing in those trying moments and witnessing their struggles in the darkest of days, helped me to come to the realization that there had to be a better way. It allowed me to discover the tactics and strategies outlined in this book and begin protecting families from suffering the same fate. My former clients have become the inspiration for better serving, educating, and empowering my community on how to keep their family out of court and out of conflict.

To my wife, Kristin: I am eternally grateful for you. You are an amazing mother, my partner in life (and crime), my confidante, my best friend, and love. This book and my career wouldn't be possible without you and your support, not only as my wife, but also as the firm bookkeeper, forensic accountant, private investigator, interior designer, marketing extraordinaire, and countless other roles you've played over the years in the office and our home. Although you may never let me hear the end of it, I would like to thank you for putting up with me, as I know it isn't an easy task (lawyers, go figure). You are the most compassionate, caring, kind, and selfless person I have ever met, and I am lucky to call you my wife and the mother of my children. Through all the late nights and weekends spent at the office or tucked away in our basement writing this book over several years, it is your understanding, support and sacrifice that made this endeavor possible.

To Kaia, my beautiful baby girl: You are my greatest joy, and you mean everything to me. You are the most joyful, hilarious, bold, fearless, and strong-willed tiny dictator the world has ever seen. You are going to be a force to be reckoned with in this world. I can't wait to see who you are destined to become, my love. Just remember to always lead with joy—it is your nature and deep down, who you truly are—don't let the world, life, fear, anger, or your temporary circumstances ever take that from you.

To Baby-B #2: The day before Valentine's Day, just a week before my deadline in the final round of editing this book, your mother told me that she was pregnant with you. I could not be happier and more excited to welcome you into this world. We have a tradition in our family that we wait to find out the sex of the baby until birth, and you won't be here before this book is published, but I can't wait for my greatest surprise in life yet. I know we haven't met, but I already love you more than you will ever know.

To my right hand, paralegal, office manager, adviser, life-coach, and pseudo-therapist, Crystal: I am forever in your debt. You deserve more credit than I could ever extend for making this book and our law firm a reality. You are the only person who truly knows what it is like to walk a mile in my shoes, and for some reason, you've stuck by my side and helped me endure all the craziness, stress, and pressure that litigation required us to put up with for all those years. For that, I am forever grateful and appreciative. I consider you family, and without your help and assistance, I wouldn't be able to function. You are an amazing person. It is your kindness, generosity, selflessness, dedication, and inspiration that make this firm run. To Nick and Gloria, I apologize for stealing this wonderful woman away from you on far too many nights and weekends during our litigation years. Countless times, I told her not to adopt my craziness and perfectionist tendencies which lead to overworking, while trying to make her go home, but she wouldn't listen.

To my Dad: In reflecting on my childhood and life, you went above and beyond. You sacrificed to give us a better life and all the luxuries you weren't afforded. In your twenties and thirties, I don't know how you managed to pull off attaining Master Chief in the Navy, climbing the corporate ladder, and serving as the preacher, den leader, coach, chauffeur, and "one of the boys." It was your work ethic, drive, persistence, discipline, demand for perfection, and unrelenting pursuit of constant improvement that have made me the man that I am today. I thank you for your example, always setting the bar high and instilling the values I am proud to pass down to our future generations.

To my Mom: You have shown me the definition and embodiment of empathy, kindness, understanding, forgiveness, and patience. It is your guidance, advice, selflessness, motherly intuition, and love that have gotten me this far in life. I don't know how you survived in a house full of stubborn, demanding, egotistical men, but I love you for being an example of all the things we are not and for doing your best to try and keep us in line and walking the straight and narrow.

To my brother: Thank you for being all the things that I am not, as well as my best man, my friend, and the one who is always willing to lend a helping hand without question.

To Walter Jackoweic: You are the embodiment of a trial attorney, and you taught me more than you will ever know. I will always strive to model your confidence, decisiveness, fearlessness, and tenacity. I am forever in your debt for stepping up to help my family when we needed you most.

To Theresa Beran-Kulat (and my fellow Collaborative Divorce Illinois colleagues): Thank you for showing me the light, positivity, and a new path. I credit you for pushing me to commit to following my new path and stop litigating. It has led me to where I am today, and I am forever grateful. Thank you for inspiring me to get out of my comfort zone and always pointing out the many available options and approaches that I had never considered. I look forward to our future work in establishing a center devoted to helping families and their children navigate the difficulties of divorce in a healthy, respectful, and dignified manner.

To my NLBM family: Without this group of like-minded, caring, generous, heart-centered, wonderful, and amazing attorneys, I wouldn't have discovered my passion to practice and serve my clients in a meaningful way, as their family's trusted adviser and personal family lawyer for life. My deepest gratitude and thanks goes out to Ali Katz, Yaasha Saaba, Lindsay Chrisler, Allison Osborn, Kevin Hermann, Jess Séguin, Don Gary, Klea Harris, A.J. Yolofsky, and all my fellow PFLs, a few of which I'm sure will now be lifelong friends, for continually inspiring, educating, and challenging me to create the life and law practice that I love.

My sincerest and deepest appreciation to Bob and Carolyn Rowley. Without your generosity, wisdom, and guidance throughout the editing process, this book wouldn't have been the same, and I am forever in your debt. I thank you for putting up with my incessant questions and requests for feedback on far too many drafts of this book. You went above and beyond, and I am eternally grateful to you for putting so much time into helping (and arguing with) me over every line, multiple times, and treating me like a member of the family. It's as if I had a second set of pseudo-parents and in-laws.

I also want to thank Eden Strong, Emily Heneghan, and all my friends and family who helped me along the way over a few years of writing this book.

To Melanie Herschorn: You are my ambassador of kwan—and you are right that no one under forty will get that reference because as much as I may not like it, I am getting old. But, in all seriousness, you were the missing piece I needed to finally bring this book to life, and I can't thank you and your team enough. I respect and admire you in so many ways, not just for what you do and all your help, but for who you are: a joy to be around, comfortable in your own skin, confident, and able to communicate and deliver a message with a kind and calm authority that makes people lean in. You embody professionalism and warmth—two traits that I only wish I could emulate—and you make it look effortless. Thank you for your leadership, guidance, honesty, and inspiration to find the best version of my voice on the page and for the future of my firm.

To my closest family, friends, coworkers, colleagues, mentors, teachers, and loved ones (you know who you are): You mean more to me than you will ever know. You have made my life worthwhile, and I truly love each and every one of you.

ABOUT THE AUTHOR

Michael Biederstadt is an attorney, author, speaker, certified mediator, and the founder of Family, Wealth & Legacy Legal Solutions, serving families across Illinois. His work sits at the intersection of estate planning, collaborative law, and family protection, helping clients make informed legal decisions and prepare accordingly, before crisis forces them into costly and adversarial outcomes.

A graduate of Loyola University Chicago, Michael earned his Juris Doctor in an accelerated 2½-year program from Valparaiso School of Law. Early in his career, he gained broad legal experience working with the Illinois State Attorney's Office prosecuting Class X felonies, clerking for the Honorable John R. Pera, contributing to the Indiana Supreme Court's statewide jury instructions and to the Indiana Rules of Civil Procedure, and representing both Olympic and collegiate athletes.

Michael spent nearly two decades in traditional family law where he witnessed firsthand the emotional, financial, and long-term impact of litigation, particularly on children caught up in the controversy. That experience led him to reevaluate the role attorneys play in perpetuating conflict within an adversarial legal system. Determined to offer a better path, he became a certified mediator and trained in collaborative law and estate planning, shifting his focus from reactive litigation to proactive strategy, proper planning and preparation.

Today, Michael is committed to helping families address what he identifies as life's most common legal problems: death, disability, and divorce, through education and thoughtful planning. He is the creator of the Family, Wealth and Legacy Plan™, Children's Protection Plan™, Generational Asset Protection Plan™, and the S.M.A.R.T. Divorce Framework™, all designed to keep families out of court, out of conflict, and aligned to achieve long-term success, regardless of what the future may hold for their family.

Michael is a devoted husband and father who enjoys reading, traveling, scuba diving, hiking, personal development, as well as studying the markets and finance.

www.ingramcontent.com/pod-product-compliance
Lightning Source LLC
LaVergne TN
LVHW100137061126
851857LV00010B/126
* 9 7 9 8 9 9 3 9 9 8 9 0 9 *